CAMBRIDGE LIBRARY COLLECTION

Books of enduring scholarly value

British and Irish History, Seventeenth and Eighteenth Centuries

The books in this series focus on the British Isles in the early modern period, as interpreted by eighteenth- and nineteenth-century historians, and show the shift to 'scientific' historiography. Several of them are devoted exclusively to the history of Ireland, while others cover topics including economic history, foreign and colonial policy, agriculture and the industrial revolution. There are also works in political thought and social theory, which address subjects such as human rights, the role of women, and criminal justice.

The Life of Mrs Godolphin

John Evelyn (1620–1706), a founder member of the Royal Society, was a horticulturalist and author, best remembered for his diaries. Throughout his prolific writings he exhibits a strong distaste for the corruption of life at court. The beautiful and pious Margaret Godolphin (1652–78), a courtier more than thirty years Evelyn's junior, with whom he struck up an intense friendship in 1672, was maid of honour in the household of Queen Catherine, wife of King Charles II. To Evelyn she represented the antithesis of the corruption he despised. Written as 'a record of her perfections' following her death in childbirth, this hagiographic biography reflects the extent of Evelyn's devotion. Left among his unrevised manuscripts, it was not published until 1847, nearly two centuries after its composition. Edited by the bishop and orator Samuel Wilberforce (1805–73), the work includes helpful notes and genealogical tables that elucidate the text.

T0381895

Cambridge University Press has long been a pioneer in the reissuing of out-of-print titles from its own backlist, producing digital reprints of books that are still sought after by scholars and students but could not be reprinted economically using traditional technology. The Cambridge Library Collection extends this activity to a wider range of books which are still of importance to researchers and professionals, either for the source material they contain, or as landmarks in the history of their academic discipline.

Drawing from the world-renowned collections in the Cambridge University Library and other partner libraries, and guided by the advice of experts in each subject area, Cambridge University Press is using state-of-the-art scanning machines in its own Printing House to capture the content of each book selected for inclusion. The files are processed to give a consistently clear, crisp image, and the books finished to the high quality standard for which the Press is recognised around the world. The latest print-on-demand technology ensures that the books will remain available indefinitely, and that orders for single or multiple copies can quickly be supplied.

The Cambridge Library Collection brings back to life books of enduring scholarly value (including out-of-copyright works originally issued by other publishers) across a wide range of disciplines in the humanities and social sciences and in science and technology.

The Life of
Mrs Godolphin

JOHN EVELYN
EDITED BY
SAMUEL WILBERFORCE

CAMBRIDGE
UNIVERSITY PRESS

CAMBRIDGE UNIVERSITY PRESS

Cambridge, New York, Melbourne, Madrid, Cape Town,
Singapore, São Paolo, Delhi, Mexico City

Published in the United States of America by Cambridge University Press, New York

www.cambridge.org
Information on this title: www.cambridge.org/9781108061940

© in this compilation Cambridge University Press 2013

This edition first published 1847
This digitally printed version 2013

ISBN 978-1-108-06194-0 Paperback

Engraved by W. Humphreys.

Mrs Godolphin

From an Original Painting in the Collection at Wootton

LONDON. WILLIAM PICKERING, 1847.

THE LIFE OF
MRS. GODOLPHIN

BY JOHN EVELYN

OF WOOTTON ESQ.

Now firſt publiſhed and
Edited by SAMUEL Lord Biſhop of OXFORD
Chancellor of the Moſt Noble
Order of the Garter

LONDON
WILLIAM PICKERING
1847

To His Grace

E D W A R D,

Lord Archbifhop of York, Lord High
Almoner, &c.

My Lord Archbishop,

*YOUR Grace will, I truft, allow
me to infcribe the following
pages to you.*

*Your unmerited kindnefs, fhown
to me on many other occafions, entrufted them to me for publication;
and I well know that whilft your
Grace has felt that the light of fuch
an example as they exhibit ought not
to be concealed, you rejoice to know
that*

*that you have lived to ſee a Britiſh
Court which in purity of morals and
domeſtic virtue affords the moſt bleſſed
contraſt to thoſe evil days through
which Margaret Godolphin was en-
abled to live in the brightneſs of a
godly purity, and to die in peace.*

    I have the honour to be,

       Your Grace's obliged and

          affeᴄtionate

             S. Oxon :

Cuddeſdon Palace,
   Feb. 1847.

Introduction.

THE following Memoir was drawn up by the accomplifhed John Evelyn, of Wootton, and intended by him for publication; but it never received his final corrections. In a manufcript paper of memoranda left at Wootton in Mr. Evelyn's hand-writing, its title occurs in a lift of " Things I would write out faire and reform if I had the leifure." In his family, the MS. has remained until the prefent time, having paffed into the hands of Mr. Evelyn's

Evelyn's great - great - grandfon,*
His Grace the Honourable Edward
Venables-Vernon Harcourt, Lord
Archbifhop of York, by whom it
has been entrufted for publication
to the care of the prefent Editor.
The MS. which is written with
extraordinary care and neatnefs,
and apparently in Mr. Evelyn's
own hand-writing, has been printed almoft as it ftands. The original fpelling, which is not uni-
form throughout the volume, has
been preferved wherever its
ftrangenefs did not throw fome
obfcurity over the meaning of the
paffage. A few words which here
and there were needful to com-
plete the fenfe have been conjec-
turally inferted, but always in
brackets.

* See Table V. p. 265.

The

The text is illuftrated by two genealogical tables, a fhort fketch of the life of Sir George Blagge, and a valuable body of illuftrative notes, which the Editor owes to the accurate and well-furnifhed pen of John Holmes, Efq. of the Britifh Mufeum, who has kindly contributed them to this volume.

From the genealogical table it will be feen, that Mrs. Godolphin fprang from an ancient and honourable houfe, and that her blood ftill flows in the veins of fome of the moft illuftrious of the nobility of England. Her hufband, who rofe to the higheft honours of the ftate, was early left a widower, and, furviving his wife thirty-four years, never remarried. He tranf-mitted to Francis, their only child, the earldom of Godolphin. This Francis,

Francis, 2nd Earl of Godolphin, married Henrietta Churchill, eldeſt daughter and co-heir of John Duke of Marlborough, to whom in her own right paſſed the dukedom of Marlborough. By the death without iſſue of William Godolphin, firſt, Viſcount Rialton, and afterwards, Marquis of Blandford,—their only ſon who attained to manhood,—the honours of the houſe of Marlborough paſſed to the family of Spencer from the deſcendants of Margaret Godolphin. By the marriage of Mary the heireſs of the 2nd Lord Godolphin to Thomas the 4th Duke of Leeds, her name and blood paſſed into the ſucceſſion of that illuſtrious houſe.

But it was not for gentle deſcent or noble alliance that Margaret

garet Godolphin was the moſt re-
markable or beſt deſerves remembrance. Rather did ſhe add dif-
tinction to an ancient line, and
tranſmit to all her poſterity that
memory of her virtues and inhe-
ritance of good deeds without
which titles and hereditary rank
are but ſplendid contradictions and
conſpicuous blemiſhes.

Her lot was caſt in the darkeſt
age of England's morals; ſhe
lived in a court where flouriſhed
in their rankeſt luxuriance all the
vice and littleneſs, which the envy
of detractors without, has ever
loved to impute—and at times,
thank God, with ſuch utter falſe-
hood—to courts in general.

In the reign of Charles the Second, that revulſion of feeling
which affects nations juſt as it
does

does individuals had plunged into diffipation all ranks on their efcape from the narrow aufterities and gloomy fournefs of puritanifm. The court, as was natural, fhared to the full in thefe new exceffes of an unreftrained indulgence; whilft many other influences led to its wider corruption. The foreign habits contracted in their banifh-ment by the returning courtiers were ill fuited to the natural gra-vity of Englifh manners, and in-troduced at once a wide-fpread licentioufnefs. The perfonal cha-racter, moreover of the King help-ed on the general corruption. Gay, popular, and witty, with a tem-per nothing could crofs, and an affability nothing could reprefs, he was thoroughly fenfual, felfifh, and depraved—vice in him was

made

made fo attractive by the wit and
gaiety with which it was tricked
out, that its utmoft groffnefs feemed for the time rather to win than
to repulfe beholders. Around the
King cluftered a band of congenial
fpirits, a galaxy of corruption, who
fpread the pollution upon every
fide. The names of Buckingham
and Rochefter, of Etheridge, Lyt-
telton, and Sedley, ftill maintain a
bad preeminence in the annals of
Englifh vice. As far as the common
eye could reach there was little to
refift the evil. The Duke of York,
the next heir to the throne, a cold-
hearted libertine, fhared the vices
of the King, without the poor
glofs of his focial attractions. It
was the day of England's deepeft
degradation, when in private life
morality was a reproach, truth departed

parted, and religion a jeft; when in affairs of ftate French gold and foreign influence had corrupted and fubdued the throned monarch, and England's King was daily lofing what had been gained by the Protector of the Commonwealth.

It was a day of heartlefs merriment, upon which fell fuddenly a night of blacknefs, which fwallowed up its crew of godlefs revellers. A picture more deeply tragical than that thus fimply fketched by Mr. Evelyn at the end, of Charles himfelf, can fcarcely be conceived. " I can never forget the inexpreffible luxury and prophanenefs, gaming and all diffolutenefs, and as it were total forgetfulnefs of God (it being Sunday evening) which this day fe'nnight

I was

I was witnefs of, the King fitting and toying with his concubines, Portfmouth, Cleaveland, and Mazarine, &c. a French boy finging love fongs in that glorious gallery, whilft about 20 of the great courtiers and other diffolute perfons were at Baffet round a large table, a bank of at leaft 2000 in gold before them, upon which two gentlemen who were with me made reflexions with aftonifhment. Six days after was all in the duft."

Evelyn's Diary, Feb. 1684-5.

In the midft of fuch a general reign of wickednefs, it is moft refrefhing to the wearied fpirit to find by clofer fearch fome living witneffes for truth and holinefs—
fome

some who, through God's Grace, passed at His call their vexed days amongst the orgies of that crew, as untainted by its evils, as is the clear sunbeam by the corruption of a loathsome atmosphere. Such an one was Margaret Godolphin, whom neither the license of those evil days, nor the scandal and detraction with which they abounded, ever touched in spirit or in reputation. Verily she walked in the flames of " the fiery furnace and felt no hurt, neither did the smell of fire pass upon her."

In what strength she lived this life the following pages will declare. They will shew that ever by her side, conversing with her spirit through its living faith, there was a fourth form like unto the Son of God. And one thing for

our

our inſtruction and encouragement
may here be ſpecially noted : that
in that day of reproach ſhe was a
true daughter of the Church of
England. Puritaniſm did not con-
tract her ſoul into moroſeneſs ; nor
did ſhe go to Rome to learn the
habits of devotion. In the train-
ing of our own Church ſhe found
enough of God's teaching to in-
ſtruct her ſoul; in its leſſons ſhe
found a rule of holy ſelf-denying
obedience ; in its prayers a practice
of devotion ; in its body a fellow-
ſhip with ſaints ; in its ordinances
a true communion with her God
and Saviour; which were able to
maintain in ſimple, unaffected purity her faith at court, in dutiful,
active love her married life ; which
ſufficed to crown her hours of bitter
anguiſh and untimely death with a
joyful

joyful refignation and affured wait-
ing for her crown.

Such is the fketch prefented in
thefe pages to the reader. May
he in a better day learn in fecret,
for himfelf, thofe leffons of heavenly wifdom which adorned the
life and glorified the death of Margaret Godolphin.

The Life of Mrs. Godolphin.

Vn Dieu vn Amy.

Madam,

I AM not vnmindfull of what your Ladyſhip lately ſug-geſted to me concerning that bleſſed Saint now in heaven. Doe you beleive I need be incited to preſerve the memory of one whoſe Image is ſoe deeply printed in my heart? Butt you would have a more permanent Record of her perfections, and ſoe would I; not onely for the veneration wee beare her precious Aſhes, butt for the

the good of thofe who, emulous of her vertues, would purfue the Inftance of it, in this, or perhapps any age before it. 'Tis certaine the materialls I have by me would furnifh one who were Mafter of a Stile becomeing foe admirable a Subject; and wifh'd I have, a thoufand tymes, the perfon in the world who knew her beft, and moft fhe loved, would give vs the picture his pencill could beft delineat : if fuch an Artift as he is decline the vndertakeing, for fear that even with all his fkill he fhould not reach the orriginall, how farr fhort am I like to fall, who cannot pretend to the meaneft of his Talents. But as indignation (they fay) fometymes creats a poem where there is no naturall difpofition in the compofer ; foe a mighty obligation, a holy freindfhipp, and your Ladyfhipp's comands, irrefiftibly prevaile with me rather to hazard the cenfure of my Imperfections, then to difobey you, or fuffer thofe precious memoryes

moryes to be loft which deferve con-
fecration to Eternity : 'tis then the leaft
and laft fervice I can exprefs to a dyeing freind for whome I fhould not have
refufed even to dye my felfe. Butt,
Madam, you will not expect I fhould
be foe exactly particular in the minuter
circumftances of her birth and what paft
in her Infancy and more tender years,
becaufe, [though] I have fometimes told
her pleafantly I would write her life,
when God knowes I little thought of
furviveing her whome often I have
wifhed might be att the clofeing of myne
owne Eyes, I had not the honor of being
acquainted with her till the laft feaven
years of her life ; I fay the little expectation I had of erecting to her a monument of this nature, made me not foe
Induftrious to Informe myfelfe of what
was paft as I fhould have beene, for I
am perfwaded that from the begining
fomething of exterordnary remarkeable
was all along confpicuous in her ; nor
was

was it poffible that my admiration of
her vertues, when I came to know her,
fhould not have prompted me to en-
quire concerneing many particulars of
her life before I. knew her; fomething
I learned cafually converfing with her,
diverfe things from the papers comunicated to me fince her deceafe, and
from what your Ladyfhipp has In-
formed me; from whome I might derive ample matter to furnifh vpon this
fubject; butt, as I faid, it would become a fteadier hand, and the penn of
an Angells wing to defcribe the life of
a Saint, who is now amongft thofe Illuftrious orders: butt, Madam, 'tis your
peremptorye Comand, I fhould fett
downe what I know, and how diffident
foever I ought to be of acquitting my
felfe as I fhould, yett fince 'tis hardly
poffible to fay any thing foe indifferently, butt muft raife an Emulation in
thofe that read or hear of it to Imitate her
vertues, [I enter] vpon the adventure.
Where

Where this excellent Creature was borne, I have learned from you ; when, from her felfe; namely, as I remember, on the Second of Auguſt, in the year 1652 ; a month and a year never to be forgotten by me without a mixture of different paſſions, for then had I born that Child whoſe early hopes yoú have often heard me deplore the loſs of, nor doe I yett remember him without emotion.

'Tis not to informe your Ladyſhipp of a thing you doe not know, butt for methods ſake that I ſpeake ſomething of the family of this Lady, which was very honorable; her father was Collonell Thomas Blagge, a Gent. of an ancient Suffolke family, and a perſon of ſoe exterordnary witt and ſignall Loyalty, as not only made him eſteemed by that bleſſed Martyr Charles the Firſt, being made Groome of his Bédd Chamber, butt to
be

be intrufted with one of his principall
Garrifons, namely that of Wallingford,
dureing the late rebellion. How wor-
thyly he acquitted himfelefe of that
charge in that vnhappy warr is vpon
another monumentall Record. Hee
lived to fee his Majeftye who now
raignes reftored to his Kingdomes and
to dye in his favour. Mrs. Blagge his
Lady (Mother to our Saint) was a woman foe eminent in all the vertues and
perfections of her fex, that it were hard
to fay whether were fuperior her Beauty, Witt, or Piety ; for, as I have heard
from thofe who intimately knew her,
fhe was in all thefe very like her daughter, and then I am fure there could nothing be added to render her a moft
admirable perfon. The iniquitye of the
tymes had accquainted her with forrow
enough to have diftracted her, being
left butt in difficult circumftances, yett
fhe lived to difcharge all her hufbands
engagements that were very confiderable

able, and to provide an honourable competency for noe lefs then 3 young daughters, whereof this was the youngeft.

Itt was by this excellent mother that this rare child was as early inftituted in the fear of God as fhe could fpeake: and as her exterordnary difcernment foone advanced to a great and early fence of Religion, foe fhe brought her to be confirmed by the now Lord Bifhopp of Ely, Doctor Gunning, who itt appeares was foe furprized att thofe early Graces he difcovered in her, thát he thought fitt fhe fhould be admitted to the holy Sacrament when fhe was hardly Eleaven years of Age: from that moment forwards, young and fprightfull as fhe was, fhe was obferved to live with great circumfpection, prefcribeing to herfelfe a conftant method of devotion, and certaine dayes of abftinence, that fhe might the better vacate to holy dutyes

dutyes and gaine that maftery over her appetite, which, with all other paffions, fhe had ftrangely fubdued to my often admiration. Butt I fhould have told your Ladyfhipp, though I remember not on what occafion, fhe went with the old Dutchefs of Richmond into France, who confign'd her to the care of the late Countefs of Guilford, Groome of the Stoole to the late Queens Mother, with whome fhe continued till her Majeftye came into England: And this minds me of what I have heard, that being frequently tempted by that Bygott profeliteffe to goe to Maffe and be a papift, our young Saint would not only not be perfwaded to it, but afferted her better faith with fuch readinefs and conftancy, (as according to the argument of that keen Religion) caufed her to be rudely treated and menaced by the Countefs; foe as fhe was become a Confeffor and almoft a Martyr before fhe was 7 years old. This paffage

fage I have from her felfe and fhe would relate it with pretty circumftances: but long ftaid fhe not in France; when being returned to her mother, fhe lived with her fometyme in London, till the raigneing peftilence of Sixty-five breakeing out, every body retireing into the Country, fhe accompanyed her into Suffolke amongft her fathers Relations there, and paft the Recefs with foe much order and fatisfaction, that with exterordnary regrett fhe was taken notice of to quitt it; when being demanded by the then Dutchefs of Yorke for a Maid of Honour, her Mother was prevailed with to place her little Daughter att Court. This was indeed a furprizeing change of Aire, and a perilous Climate, for one foe very young as fhe, and fcarcely yett attained to the twelvth year of her age: butt by how much more the danger foe much greater the virtue and difcretion which not only preferved her fteady in that giddy Station,

tion, but foe improv'd, that the example of this little Saint influenced not
onely her honourable companions, butt
fome who were advanc'd in yeares before her, and of the moft illuftrious
quality. What! fhall I fay, fhe like a
young Apoftlefs began to plant Religion in that barren Soyle? Arethufa
paff'd thro' all thofe turbulent waters
without foe much as the leaft ftaine or
tincture in her Chriftall, with her Piety
grew vp her Witt, which was foe fparkling, accompanyed with a Judgment
and Eloquence foe exterordnary, a
Beauty and Ayre foe charmeing and
lovely, in a word, an Addrefs foe vniverfally takeing, that after few years, the
Court never faw or had feen fuch a
Conftellation of perfections amongft all
their fplendid Circles. Nor did this,
nor the admiration it created, the Elogies fhe every day received, and appli-
cation of the greateft perfons, at all elate
her; fhe was ftill the fame, allwayes in
perfect

perfect good humour, allwayes humble,
allwayes Religious to exactnefs. Itt
rendred her not a whitt morofs, tho'
fometymes more ferious, cafting ftill
about how fhe might continue the
houres of publique and private devotion and other exercifes of piety, to
comply with her duty and attendance
on her Royall Miftrefs without fingularity or Reproach.

Thus paff'd fhe her tyme in that
Court till the Dutchefs dyed, dureing
whofe Sicknefs, accompanyed (as it
was) with many vncomfortable circumftances, fhe waited and attended with
an exterordnary fedulity, and as fhe has
fometymes told me, when few of the
reft were able to endure the fatigue:
and therefore here, before I proceed, I
cannot but take notice of thofe holy
and exterordnary reflections fhe made
vpon this occafion, as I find them
amongft other loofe papers vnder her
owne

owne faire hand, when compareing her dear Mothers ſickneſs and other freinds departure with that of the Dutcheſs, thus ſhe writes.

" Mrs. N. dead, was an example of patience vnder a burthen that was well nigh vnſupportable ; often ſhe received the bleſſed Sacrament, often ſhe prayed and was very much reſign'd, not ſurprized nor in confuſion, but perceiveing her ſight decay, calling vpon God after many holy and pious diſcourſes and exhortations, ſhe calmely bidd her freinds farewell.

" A poore woman dead, worne to ſkyn and bones with a conſumption, ſhe made noe Complaints, but truſted in God, and that what he thought fitt was beſt, and to him reſign'd her ſoule. A poore creature that had been a great ſinner, died in miſſerable paines, in exceeding terror ; God was gracious to her,

her, ſhe was patient, very devout, ſhe was
releaſed in prayer. My mother dead,
at firſt ſurprized, and very unwilling;
ſhe was afterwards reſign'd, received
often, prayed much, had holy things
read to her, delighted in heavenly diſcourſe, deſired to be diſſolv'd and be
with Chriſt, ended her life chearfully,
and without paine, left her family in
order and was much lamented.

"The D - - dead, a princeſs honoured in power, had much witt, much
mony, much eſteeme; ſhe was full of
vnſpeakable tortur, and died (poore
creature) in doubt of her Religion,
without the Sacrament, or divine by
her, like a poore wretch; none remem-
bred her after one weeke, none ſorry
for her; ſhe was toſt and flung about,
and every one did what they would
with that ſtately carcaſe. What is this
world, what is greatneſs, what to be eſteemed, or thought a witt? Wee ſhall
all

all be ſtript without ſence or remembrance. But God, if wee ſerve him in
our health, will give vs patience in our
Sickneſs."

I repeate the inſtance as ſett downe
in her diarye, to ſhew how early ſhe
made theſe vſefull and pious Recollections, for ſhe muſt needs be then very
young, and att an age att .leaſt when
very few of her ſex, and in her circumſtances, much concerne themſelves with
theſe mortifyeing reflections. Butt, as
I have often heard her ſay, ſhe loved
to be att funeralls, and in the houſe of
mourning, ſoe being of the moſt com-
paſſionate nature in the world, ſhe was
a conſtant viſiter of the ſick and of people in diſtreſs. But, to proceed; ſhe had
not been above two yeares att Court
before her virtue, .beauty, and witt
made her be looked vpon as a little
miracle; and indeed there were ſome
addreſſes made her of the greateſt perſons

fons, not from the attraction of affected
Charmes, for fhe was ever, att that
fprightfull and free age, feverely carefull how fhe might give the leaft countenance to that liberty which the Gallants there doe vfually affume of talking with lefs referve ; nor did this ecclipfe her pretty humour, which was
chearfull and eafy amongft thofe fhe
thought worthy her converfation. Itt is
not to be difcribed (for it was tho' naturall, in her *in*imitable) with what Grace,
ready and folid vnderftanding, fhe would
difcourfe. Nothing that fhe conceived
could be better expreffed, and when fhe
was fometymes provok'd to Railly,
there was nothing in the world foe
pleafant, and inoffenfively diverting,
(fhall I fay) or inftructive ; for fhe ever
mingl'd her freeft entertainments with
fomething which tended to ferious, and
did it in fuch a manner, as allwayes left
fome impreffions exterordnary even
vpon thofe who came perhapps with inclinations

clinations to pervert the moſt harmeleſs converſations ; foe as it was impoſſible for any to introduce a ſyllable which did not comply with the ſtricteſt rules of decency.

But I ſhall not be foe well able to deſcribe what I ſhould ſay vpon this occaſion, as by giveing your Ladyſhipp the meaſures which ſhe preſcrib'd her-ſelfe for the government of her Actions, when ſhe was of duty to attend vpon her Majeſtye in publique, and when it was not only impoſſible, but vnbecome-ing to entertaine thoſe who compoſed the Royall Circle, and were perſons of the moſt illuſtrious qualitye, without cenſure and rudeneſs. Behold then, Madam, what I find written in her owne hands againe, and that might be a coppy for all that ſucceed her in that honourable Station to tranſcribe and imitate it ; for ſhe kept not onely a moſt accurate account of all her actions,

tions, butt did likewife regifter her
ferious purpofes and refolutions, the
better to confirme and fix them, foe
as they were not hafty fitts of zeale and
fudden tranfports, but follemne and deliberate; and this I rather chufe to doe
alfoe in her owne very words and method, innocent, naturall, and unaffected.

"*My life, by God's Grace, without
which I can doe nothing.*

"I muft, till Lent, rife att halfe an
houre after eight a clock; whilft put-
ting on morning cloathes, fay the prayer for Death and the Te Deum: then
prefently to my prayers, and foe either
drefs my felfe or goe to Church prayers.
In dreffing, I muft confider how little
it fignifyes to the faveing of my foule,
and how foolifh 'tis to be angry about
a thing fo vnneceffary. Confider what
our Saviour fuffered.—O Lord, affift
me.

"When

" When I goe into the withdrawing
roome, lett me confider what my calling is: to entertaine the Ladys, not to
talke foolifhly to Men, more efpecially
the King; lett me confider, if a Tray-
tor be hatefull, fhe that betrayes the
foule of one is much worfe;—the danger,
the fin of it. Then without pretend-
ing to witt, how quiet and pleafant a
thing it is to be filent, or if I doe fpeake,
that it be to the Glory of God.—Lord,
affift me.

" Att Church lett me mind in what
place I am; what about to afk, even
the falvation of my foule; to whome I
fpeak,—to the God that made me, redeemed and fanctifyed me, and can yett
cutt me off when he pleafes.—O Lord,
affift me.

" When I goe to my Lady Fal-
mouths, I ought to take paines with her
about

about her Religion, or elſe I am not her freind; to ſhew example by calmneſs in diſpute, in never ſpeaking ill of anybody to her, butt excuſeing them rather.

" Goe to the Queene allwayes att nine, and then read that place concerning the drawing roome, and lett my man waite for me to bring me word before publique prayers begin. If I find ſhe dynes late, come downe, pray and read, namely, that concerning prayer; and think why I read, to benefitt my ſoule, paſs my tyme well, and improve my vnderſtanding.—O Lord, aſſiſt me.

" Be ſure ſtill to read that for the drawing roome in the privy chamber, or preſence, or other place before prayers, and ſoe againe into the drawing room for an hour or ſoe; and then ſlipp to my chamber and divert myſelfe in reading ſome pretty booke, becauſe the
Queen

Queen does not require my waiteing ;
after this to fupper, which muft not be
much if I have dyned well ; and att
neither meale to eate above two difhes,
becaufe temperance is beft both for
foule and body; then goe vpp to the
Queen, haveing before read, and well
thought of what you have written.
Amen.

" Sett not vp above halfe an hour
after eleaven att moft ; and as you vn-
drefs, repeate that prayer againe ; butt
before, confider that you are perhapps
goeing to fleepe your laft; being in bedd
repeate your hymne foftly, ere you
turne to fleepe.

" If I awake in the night lett me fay
that (for which fhe had collected many
excellent paffages, as I find among her
papers,) pfalm.   Lord, affift me.

" In the morning, wakeing, vfe a fhort
devotion,

devotion, and then as foone as ever you awake, rife imediately to praife him. The Lord affift me."

In another place of the fame Diarye, about which tyme I fuppofe there was fome play to be acted by the maids of honour.—"Now as to pleafure, they are fpeaking of playes and laughing att devout people; well, I will laugh att myfelfe for my impertinencyes, that by degrees I may come to wonder why any body does like me; and divert the difcourfe; and talke of God and moralitye: avoid thofe people when I come into the drawing roome, efpecially among great perfons to divert them; becaufe noe raillary allmoft can be innocent: goe not to the Dutchefs of Monmouth above once a weeke, except when wee drefs to rehearfe, and then carry a booke along with me to read when I don't act, and foe come away before fupper.

" Talke

"Talke little when you are there; if they fpeak of any body I can't commend, hold my peace, what jeft foever they make; be fure never to talk to the King; when they fpeak filthyly, tho' I be laugh'd att, looke grave, remembring that of Micha, there will a tyme come when the Lord will bind vp his jewells. Never meddle with others buifnefs, nor hardly afk a queftion; talk not flightly of religion. If you fpeake any thing they like, fay 'tis borrowed, and be humble when commended. Before I fpeake, Lord, affift me; when I pray, Lord, heare me; when I am praifed, God, humble me; may the clock, the candle, every thing I fee, inftruct me; Lord cleanfe my hands, lett my feete tread thy pathes. Is any body laughed att, fay it may be my cafe; is any in trouble, fay, 'Lord, in juftice I deferve it; butt thou art all mercy; make me thankfull.' On Feftivall evens I refolve to dyne att home, and to repeat

peat all the pſalmes I know by heart,"
(of which ſhe had almoſt the whole pſal-
ter,) " reſerveing my reading or part of
my prayers till night; and ſupp with
bread and beere only.

" On Frydayes and Wedneſdaies
I'le eat nothing till after evening prayer;
and ſoe come downe as ſoone as ever
the Queene has dyned, without goeing
to viſitt, till my owne prayers are finiſhed.

" The ſame will I obſerve the day
before I receive; vſe to pray on thoſe
dayes by daylight; and early on Sundayes, and think of no diverſion till after
evening prayer; to dyne abroad as
little as poſſible, but performe my conſtant duty to God and the Queene.
Aſſiſt me, O Lord; Amen.

" Sing Pſalmes now and then out of
Sundayes. Endeavour to begg with
teares

teares what you afke, and O lett them be, O Lord, my onely pleafure. There are 3 Sundayes to come from this Saturday night; pray one day earneftly to God for love, and againft takeing his name in vaine, pray againft intemperance and fenfuality; and the other day for meekenefs, and againft envy; another for fear and alliance, and againft detraction.

"I have vowed, if it be poffible, not to fett vpp paft ten a clock; therefore, before you engage in company, goe downe and read this, and be as much alone as you can; and when you are abroad talke to men as little as may be : carry your prayer booke in your pockett, or any thing that may decently keepe you from converfeing with men."

Behold what this bleffed faint had promifcuoufly fett downe in her diary att feverall tymes, as refolutions made

vpon

vpon feverall occafions, all of them
tending to the inftitution of her life in
a courfe of exterordnary and early piety,
for fhe was now very young, and I,
therefore, give them your Ladyfhipp
in her owne method, without method
or ftudied connexion : nor are thefe the
firft I have feene of hers in this nature.
She did vpon feverall occurrences record her purpofes, and what fhe foe refolved fhe punctually perform'd. Butt
with what exterordnary caution fhe
govern'd herfelf att Court; how holy,
innocent, inftructive, and vfefull, her
intire converfation was; how much fhe
improved in virtue, and made devotion
the pleafure as well as imployment of
her tyme, I need not tell your Ladyfhipp : nor vfed fhe to trick and drefs
herfelfe vpp, tho' in foe fplendid and
vaine a theater, to the purpofes of vanity,
or to be fine and ador'd : fhe was extreamly fhy of talking among the gallants and young men, to pafs away the
tedioufnefs

tedioufnefs of attendance; nor made
fhe impertinent vifitts; for fhe had fill'd
vp the whole day, and deftin'd almoft
every minute of it to exercife. When,
therefore, I have fum'd vp all, and confider'd well how much of it all I have
feene, and how with it all fhe preferved the lively and elegant converfation which rendered her foe infinitely
agreeable to all that knew her, I cannot butt redouble my admiration and
efpecially how often and fenfible fhe
has difcourfed with me concerning the
wonderfull fatisfaction fhe tooke in the
dutyes of Religion.

Butt here, before I proceed any further, the method of tyme, and other
circumftances require me to fay fomething how I came to be firft acquainted
with this excellent creature, and by
what tyes of facred freindfhipp I find
my felfe foe highly obliged to celebrate
her memory; and this I fhall doe the
rather

rather becaufe the Lord has foe great
a part in itt, that without ingratitude,
I may not pafs it over; nor is it without frefh delight that I ftill call to mind
thofe innocent dayes, and the fweet
converfation which fifteene yeares fince
wee enjoyed, that our familyes being
neare to one another, gave vs the
happynefs to be knowne to the moft
obligeing neighbour in the world; from
foe long a date it is that my wife com-
putes her firft haveing had the blefling
of begining an acquaintance with Mrs.
Blagge, whome your mother and fifter
fometimes kindly brought with them
to our poore villa: butt few of thofe
civilityes of cafuall or refpectfull vifitts
had paffed, before my wife had difcovered fuch exterordnary charmes, markes
of virtue and difcretion in her converfation, that fhe would often reprove the
diffidence I was wont to exprefs, when
they would fometymes difcourfe of Piety
and Religion, eminent among the Court
Ladyes,

Ladyes; and vpon which fubject your
Ladyfhipp would frequently joine with
my wife in conflict againft me, to the
reproach of my Morofenefs, and Infide-
delity, efpecially of a thing foe airy
and foe gay as fome reprefented this
miracle to me. And in this Error I had
certainly perfifted, notwithftanding I
had fometymes taken notice of her,
both att my houfe and att Church, to
be a very agreeable Lady; butt that
fhe or any body elfe in her Court circumftances, was principl'd with fuch
a folid Virtue, and did cultivate it to
that degree, I was brought to beleive
with foe much difficulty, that it was almoft Seaven yeares before your Ladyfhipp could convince me. You had,
indeed, a Sifter there, whofe perfections would no longer fuffer me to continue alltogeather in this falfe perfwa-
fion; butt to beleive there were many
Saints in that Country I was not much
inclined; nor likely had chang'd that
                              opinion

opinion, if an Imployment had not of neceſſity ſometymes obliged me to come from my Receſs, when I as little affected to be knowne and to multiply acquaintance of that ſex as another man. I minded my Bookes and my Garden, and the Circle was bigg enough for me. I aſpir'd to no offices, noe titles, no favours att Court, and really was hardly knowne to thoſe next neighbours of mine, whome I had lived allmoſt twenty years by: butt the Country where this Lady lived I had much more averſion to, for the reaſons you may gueſs, and which made her quitt it aſſoone as ſhe could. 'Twas, I ſay, about a year that ſhe had ſometymes beene att my houſe, when your Ladyſhipp came to hector me out of my contracted humour, but I continually return'd to it; and when, by Chance, you att any tyme nam'd her, I fancied her ſome airy thing, that had more Witt than Diſcretion; till vpon your

Ladyſhipp

Ladyſhipp and my Wifes more ſe-
verely reproaching me for being ſcarcely
civill to a Companion of your excellent Siſters, for whome I had much eſteeme, (though butt little acquainted)
I found my ſelfe oblig'd, in good manners, to waite vpon her when I came
to Whitehall. I ſpeake of the Lady,
your Siſter, then Maid of Honour ; for
I would objeᴄt, that there was a Witt
with her whome I feared, and that I
was the moſt unfitt perſon in the world
for the entertainments of the Anti
Chamber, and the little Spiritts that
dwell in Fairy Land. You aſſured me
ſhe was humble and Religious, and extreamly ſerious, and that [if] I would beleive you, I ſhould not be diſpleaſed with
the adventure ; for tho' ſhe had abundance of Witt, and rallied ſhrewdly,
yett ſhe was civill and diſcreete, and
exterordnary obligeing. Vpon this, I
made your Siſter a viſitt, and ſurprized
Mrs. Blagge, who it ſeems that day
was

was dreff'd for Audience and Cere-
mony, vpon which I would have with-
drawne, butt her Chamber fellow ftaid
me, and I was not vnwilling to hear
her talke; butt I fince came to under-
ftand, it was a day of folemn devotion
with her, and fhe excufed her felfe, faid
little, and look'd very humble, which
I liked, and foe for this tyme, tooke
my leave.

I concluded by this fhe might not be
that pert Lady I had fancyed; and fhe
afterwards fpake curteoufly to me,
cafually meeting her in the houfe, and
that fhe hoped fhe had not frighted me
from her apartment. I came once or
twice after this with my wife to vifitt
your Sifter; when this Lady keepeing
her Chamber caufed me one day to
dyne with her, which I tooke kindly,
becaufe 'twas without affectation and
with no danger of furfeiting. Butt her
converfation was a treat, and I began
to

to admire her temperance, and tooke
efpeciall notice, that however wide or
indifferent the fubject of our difcourfe
was amongft the reft, fhe would allwayes
divert it to fome Religious conclufion ;
and foe temper and feafon her Replyes,
as fhew'd a gratious heart, and that fhe
had a mind wholly taken vp with heavenly thoughts.

After this introduction fhe conjur'd
me not to baulk her holy Cell, and I
was not a little pleafed to be foe folemnly diverted and find my felfe mif-
taken, that foe young, foe elegant, foe
charming a Witt and Beauty fhould
preferve foe much Virtue in a place
where it neither naturally grew nor
much was cultivated ; for with all thefe
perfections, Vivacitye and Apprehen-
tion beyond what I could expect, fhe
feemed vnconcerned and fteady, could
endure to be ferious, and gently reprove
my Moroffnefs, and was greatly devout,

vout, which putt me out of all feare of her Railary, and made me looke vpon her with exterordnary refpeĉt. Thus every vifitt abated of my prejudice: her difcourfes were not trifleing and effe-minate, butt full of Virtue and mate-riall, and of a moft tender regard to Religion. Butt itt was after your Lady-fhipps Mother was gone into Lincoln-fheir, and had carryed away her com-panion, that fhe told me, " now Mrs. Howard is gone, fhe beleived fhe fhould have little of my Company; butt if I were not weary of her, and would be foe charitable, fhe fhould take it kindly that I came often to her." This was a Compliment you know I needed not, for by this tyme I was foe well affured of her Inclinacion to Goodnefs, that fhe could not imagine me capable of neg-lecting a perfon from whofe converfa-tion I never return'd butt with advan-tage. I foone perceived what touched me to the heart, and that was her foule; and

and how her Inclinacions pointed to
God; that her difcourfes, defignes, and
actions tended allwayes thither: and
other obfervations which I made to my
exterordnary wonder and admiracion.
This Creature (would I fay to my
felfe) loves God; 'tis a thoufand pittyes
butt fhe fhould perfift; what a new thing
is this, I think Paulina and Euftochius are come from Bethlehem to Whitehall; and from this moment I began to
looke vpon her as facred, and to blefs
God for the graces which fhoone in her.
I dayly prayed for her as fhe had en-
joined me, and fhe began to open fome
of her holy thoughts to me; and I faw
a flagrant devotion, and that fhe had
totally refigned herfelfe to God; and
with thefe Incentiues, who, that had
any fence of Religion, could forbeare
to vallue her exceedingly?

Itt was not long after this, that being
one day to vifitt her, fhe feem'd to me
more

more thoughtfull than ordinary. I afked
her, what made her looke foe folemnly.
She told me, fhe had never a freind in
the world. Noe, faid I, thats impoffible; I beleive no body has more; for
all that know you muft love you, and
thofe that love you are continually your
freinds. Butt I, who well knew where
her heart att that tyme was, afked her
what fhe efteemed a certaine Gentleman beyond the Seas. Alas, fays fhe,
he is very ill, and that makes me very
much concerned; butt I doe not fpeake
to you of him, whome God will I hope
be gratious to, but I would have a
Freind. In that name is a great deale
more then I can exprefs, a faithfull
freind, whome I might truft with all
that I have, and God knows, that is
butt little; for him whome you meane
does not care to meddle with my concerns, nor would I give him the trouble. This, to my remembrance, were
her very expreffions to me. Madam,
faid

faid I, doe you fpeake this to me, as if
I were capable of ferving you in any
thing confiderable? I beleive you the
perfon in the world (replyed fhe) who
would make fuch a freind as I wifh for,
if I had meritt enough to deferve it.
Madam, faid I, confider well what you
fay, and what you doe, for it is fuch a
truft, and foe great an obligation that
you lay vpon me, as I ought to em-
brace with all imaginable refpect, and
acknowledgment for the greateft honour you could doe me; Madam, to be
called your freind were the moft defire-
able in the world, and I am fure I
fhould endeavour to acquitt me of the
duty with great chearfullnefs and fidelity. Pray leave your complimenting,
(faid fhe fmileing) and be my freind
then, and looke vpon me henceforth as
your Child. To this purpofe was her
obligeing reply; and there ftanding
pen and ink vpon the table, in which I
had been drawing fomething vpon a paper

per like an Alter, ſhe writt theſe words:
Be this the Symboll of Inviolable
Freindſhip,—Mary Blagge, 16th October, 1672, and vnderneath, For my
brother E - - - ; and ſoe delivered it
to me with a ſmile.   Well, ſaid I, Madam, this is an high obligation, and you
have allready paid me for the greateſt
ſervice that I can ever pretend to doe
you; butt yett doe you know what
you have done?   Yes, ſayes ſhe, very
well; butt pray what doe you meane?
Why, ſaid I, the title that has conſe-
crated this Alter is the Marriage of
Souls, and the Golden thread that tyes
the hearts of all the world; I tell you,
Madam, Freindſhipp is beyond all relations of fleſh and blood, becauſe it is
leſs materiall; there is nature in that of
parents and kindred, butt [that of]
Freindſhipp is of courſe and without
election, for which the Conjugall State it
ſelfe is not alwayes the moſt happy;
and, therefore, thoſe who have had beſt
experience

experience chuſe their freind out of all theſe circumſtances, and have found him more laſting, and more effectuall. By this Symboll you give me title to all that you can with Honour and Religion part with in this world; and it is a topic I could adorne with glorious examples of what I ſpeak; and the nobleſt things have been ſaid vpon it; and the Laws and Meaſures of Freindſhipp are the niceſt and the moſt obligeing;—but you know them all. Well, replyed ſhe, ſmileing, be it ſoe,—pray what am I to doe? Nay, ſaid I, I'll tell you firſt what you are to ſuffer.

The priviledges I claime (in virtue of that character) are that I may viſitt you without being thought importunate; that I may now and then write to you to cultivate my Stile; diſcourſe with you to improve my Vnderſtanding; read to you to receive your Reflections; and that you freely command
me

me vpon all occaſions without any re-
ſerve whatſoever: you are to write to
me when I am abſent; mention me in
all your prayers to God, to admoniſh
me of all my failings, to viſitt me in
ſickneſs, to take care of me when I am
in diſtreſs, and never to forſake me,
change or leſſen your particular eſteeme,
till I prove vnconſtant or perfidious,
and noe mans freind: in a word, there
is in Freindſhipp ſomething of all relations, and ſomething above them all.
Theſe, Madam, are the Laws, and they
are reciprocall and eternall, &c.

Thus, for a tyme, 'twixt jeſt and
earneſt, the converſation putt her into
the moſt agreeable humor in the world.
Well, ſaid ſhe, I will conſider of what
you ſay; butt pray remember you be
my freind, and when next you come,
I will tell you what I have for you to
doe in good earneſt; and a little after
writt me this Letter.

" *My*

" *My Freind,*

" I have confidered and minded well
what was faid, and what I writt, and
will not recall it. I vnderftood fomething of the office of freindfhipp before
I knew you, butt after what you have
faid and offered, I beleive I fhall need
little Inftruction. Gratitude, join'd with
the greateft efteeme I had before of you,
will require all that you mention on my
part: you are then, my firft freind, the
firft that ever I had, and ever fhall you
be foe. This is trueth vpon the word
of a Chriftian; and I beleive I fhall not
lay downe my refolution of continueing
yours butt with my life. I thankfully
accept all your Councell, and will endeavour to follow it; butt birds themfelves have allwayes the good nature
to teach their young ones, and foe muft
you; looke vpon me then as your child
as well as friend, and love me as your
child, and, if you will, call me foe.
What

What Meaſures you are to obſerve I
meddle not with ; for a friend may doe
what he pleaſes ; they who give mony,
give all : 'tis a ſaying of your owne as
to Charity, they that are friends are
all things,—lett that be myne. Butt
as for the returnes for the good offices
I receive, I beleive my advice can be of
little vſe to you, vnleſs to ſerve you as
an Act of humility, which muſt be all
the reaſon you will ever have to require
it ; what ſhall I ſay then more ? till death
reckon me your freind ; you ſee how I
think I am with you ; and now, after
all this, I may grow old or forgettfull,
and Melancholy or Stupid, and in that
Caſe, will no more anſwer for my ſelfe
then for a Stranger ; butt, whilſt I am
my ſelfe and a Chriſtian, I will be
yours."

Itt would be an vnpardonable oſten-
tation in me, and a great temptation to
over vallue my ſelfe, and the poore
ſervices

services she was pleafed to accept of,
should I here repeate what she has left
me vnder her owne hand vpon this
fubject, in the moft pious and endear-
ing expreffions that could poffibly fall
from the moft fincere and obligeing
Creature in the world : butt to lett them
pafs,—'tis certaine, that from this moment, I no more look'd vpon her as
Mrs. Blagge, butt as my child indeed,
and did, to the vttmoft of my poore
abilitye, advice and ferve her in all
her fecular and no few fpirituall affaires
and concerns, with a diligence and fidelity becomeing the truft and confidence she repofed in me, as an honour
to be envyed by the beft of men : her
friendfhipp after this to me was foe
tranfcendently fincere, noble, and Religious, as taught me all its demeanfions,
beyond any thing I ever read of its
higheft Ideas ; and she herfelfe was
heard to fay, what she once thought to
be a name onely and nothing elfe, she
found

found a reall exiftance ; and that friendfhipp was for mutuall Improvement,
and to fortifye every virtue ; and, indeed, fhe was able to direct, and Councell, and encourage, and Comfort. Nay,
and has often told me with becomeing
passion, That fhe with Joy could dye
for a friend ; vrgeing that fentence of
St. Pauls, nor are the meafures hard ;
I am fure willingly would I have done
it for her: O fweete, O how defire-
able! And, indeed, thefe holy tranfports
made the Chriftians comunicate all they
had ; the apoftles fpeake of fome who
would have pluck'd out their very eyes
and laid downe their necks for him,
and called nothing their owne which
others wanted. 'Tis this which made
thofe faints of one mind and of one
heart ; 'tis this has Crown'd a hundred
thoufand martyrs, and fhewed vs that
the moft confumate friendfhipps are the
products of Religion and the love of
God. There are Inumerable expreffions

fions of this nature to be found in her letters to me, which are Charming, and indeed, foe tender and perfonall, that, tho' one (who) knew my demeritts as well as I my felfe doe, would fufpect their fincerity ; yett I knew to be from her heart, which was full of moft generous refentments. In a word, I may fay, as David did of Jonathan, her friendfhipp to me was paffing the love of women ; nor verily, was it without an intire fimpathye on my part ; and there was providence in itt, as well as inclination for the exceeding and moft eminent piety and goodnefs that ever confecrated a worthy freindfhipp, fhone foe bright in this bleffed faint, as intitled her to all the fervices, refpect, and veneration I was capable of giveing her.

Never am I to forgett this Golden expreffion of hers to me. I would have (fayes fhe) nothing that paffes betweene vs have any Refemblance of friendfhipp friendſhipp that doe not laſt. Butt, Madam, whither has this Indearing topic tranſported me.

After this ſolemn engagement then, ſhe ſoone accquainted me with many of her concerns; made me the depoſitarie of her pious thoughts and reſolutions, and putt her whole fortune intirely into my hands; which, indeed, lay in ſome danger for want of that aſſiſtance, which ſhe might have had from an able perſon, tho' from none more faithfull and more Induſtrious to Improve it to the beſt of my capacity.; I was only greiv'd, when att any tyme ſhe thought it a trouble to me; butt ſhe would ſay: I am your Child, and whither ſhould I goe butt to you; never will I doe any thing without you whilſt I live: more difference and humility could ſhe not have paid to a father; more confidence in a friend; and this temper'd with that ſweetneſs and exterordnary

terordnary piety, that I am not able to
fupport the confideration of the lofs of
fuch a friendfhipp without vnfpeakable
griefe.

Seldome or rarely came I to waite on
her, (if fhe were not in company) but
I found her in her little oratorie, and
fome tymes all in feares, for never was
Creature more devout and tender ; and
a thoufand Cafes and queftions would fhe
propound to me, for which I would ftill
referr her to that Reverend and learn'd
divine, with whome fhe did conftantly
correfpond vpon all occafions of fpirituall
advice ; foe carefull and curious was
this faint in the concernments of her
foule ; butt fhe would often tell me,
he was too gentle, and, therefore, required of me to deale Impartially ; [that]
I was her friend, and that a friend was
Ghoftly father, and every thing to her ;
indeed I would often reprove her tire-
fome methods and thought to plant
the

the confideracion of the memory and
love of God in her thoughts; and to
cure her of the fad and frieghtfull apprehenfions fhe fometymes feemed to
have, that God was a fevere exacter;
that fhe had never done enough, and
ferved an auftere Mafter, not to be
pleafed without abundance of labour
and formes without end; and for this
fhe would frequently give me thanks,
that I had lett her fee and taft more of
the love of God and delices of Religion,
then ever fhe had before. And veryly
this holy and Religious temper of hers,
was enough to winn the efteeme of all
that had any fence of goodnefs. Nor
was her tyme wholly fpent in the contemplative part of piety; fhe was allwayes doeing fome good offices for one
or other, gave frequent and confiderable releife to poore and indigent people, and not feldome made me her almoner, and the hand to convey it where
fhe could not well her felfe; butt of
this

this and the many vifitts fhe in her
owne perfon made (delicate as fhe was)
to refrefh and comfort the fick and miferable, even amongft the moft wretch-
edly poore, nott without great inconveniency to her health, I fhall give
account hereafter : butt hitherto was
fhe advanc'd, being yett hardly enter'd
her Nineteenth yeare, an age that few in
her circumftances foe foone fett out att,
and [would] that I begun as early and as
early finifh'd.

Wee will now then looke vpon her
as att Whitehall, whither fhe came
from St. James to waite vpon her Majeftye, after the death of the Dutchefs,
when fhe was not above fixteene.   I
had not then indeed the honour to
know her ; butt I have heard from
others, that her beauty and her witt
was foe exterordinary improved, as there
had nothing been feene more furprizeing, and full of charmes ; every body
                                    was

was in love with, and fome allmoft dyeing for her, whilft with all the Modefty
and Circumfpection imaginable, fhe
ftrove to Eclipfe the lufter which fhe
gave; and would often check the vivacity
which was naturall, and perfectly became her, for feare of giveing occafion
to thofe who lay in waite to deceive.
Butt it was not poffible here to make the
leaft approach, butt fuch as was full of
Honour; and the diftance fhe obferv'd,
and Caution and Judgment fhe was
miftrefs of, protected her from all im•
pertinent addreffes, till fhe had made a
Choice, without Reproach, and worthy
her Efteeme, namely, of that excellent
Perfon, who was afterwards her Hufband, after a paffion of no lefs than
Nine long yeares, that they both had
been the moft intire and faithfull lovers
in the world. This was a fpace indeed
of fufficient probation, nor will I prefume to dive into the circumftances
which made them be foe long refolve-
ing,

ing, fhe being then it feems butt very
young, and both of a temper foe extreamly difcreete. Butt as to the firft
Impreffions, I will relate to your Ladyfhipp what I have learn'd from her
felfe, when fometymes fhe was pleafed
to truft me with diverfe paffages of her
Life. For it was not poffible I could
hear of foe long an Amour, foe honorable a love and conftant paffion, and
which I eafily perceived concerned her,
as lookeing vpon herfelfe vnfettled,
and one who had long fince refolved
nott to make the Court her reft, butt
I muft be touched with fome Care for
her. I would now and then kindly
chide her, why fhe fuffer'd thofe lan-
guifhments when I knew not on whome
to lay the blame. For tho' fhe would
induftrioufly conceale her difquiett, and
divert it vnder the notion of the Spleene,
fhe could not but acknowledge to me
where the dart was fix'd ; nor was any
thing more ingenious then what fhe
                                    now

now writt me vpon this Subject, by
which your Ladyfhipp will perceive, as
with what peculiar confidence fhe was
pleafed to honour me, foe, with what
early prudence and great pietye fhe ma-
nag'd the paffion, which, of all other,
young people are comonly the moft precipitate in and vnadvif'd.

" I came," fayes fhe, " foe young, as
I tell you, into the world (that is, about
14 yeares of Age,) where no fooner was
I entred, butt various opinions were
delivered of me and the perfon whome
(you know,) was more favourable then
the reft were to me, and did, after fome
tyme, declare it to me. The firft thing
which tempts young weomen is vanity,
and I made that my great defigne.
Butt Love foone taught me another
Leffon, and I found the trouble of
being tyed to the hearing of any fave
him ; which made me refolve that either
he or none fhould have the poffeffion
of

of your Friend. Being thus foone fencible of Love my felfe, I was eafily
perfwaded to keepe my felfe from giveing him any caufe of Jealoufye, and in
foe long a tyme never has there been
the leaft.

" This, vnder God's providence, has
been the means of preferveing me from
many of thofe mifsfortunes young Creatures meet with in the world, and in a
Court efpetially. Att firft wee thought
of nothing but liveing allwayes togeather, and that wee fhould be happy.
Butt att laft he was fent abroad by his
Majeftye, and fell fick, which gave me
great trouble ; and I allow'd more tyme
for Prayer and the performance of holy
dutyes than before I had ever done,
and I thank God, found infinite pleafure in it, farr beyond any other, and I
thought lefs of foolifh things that vfed
to take vp my tyme. Being thus changed
my felfe, and likeing it foe well, I earneftly

eftly begg'd of God that he would im-
part the fame fatisfaction to him I
loved; 'tis done, (my friend) 'tis done,
and from my foule I am thankfull;
and tho' I beleive he loves me paffionately, yett I am not where I was : my
place is fill'd vpp with HIM who is all
in all. I find in him none of that tor-
menting paffion to which I need facre-
fice my felfe; butt ftill were wee diff-
engag'd from the world, wee fhould
marry vnder fuch reftraints as were fitt,
and by the agreeablenefs of our humour, make each other happy. Butt
att prefent there are obftructions : he
muft be perpetually engaged in buiffnefs,
and follow the Court, and live allwayes
in the world, and foe have lefs tyme
for the fervice of God, which is a fenf-
cible affliction to him ; wherefore, wee
are not determined to precipitate that
matter, butt to expect a while, and fee
how things will goe; haveing a great
mind to be togeather, which cannot
with

with decency be done without marrying, nor, to either of our fatisfactions,
without being free from the world.
In fhort, ferving of God is our end,
and if wee cannott do that quietly togeather wee will afunder. You know
our Saviour fayes, that all could not
receive that doctrine, but to thofe who
could, he gave noe contradiction; and
if wee can butt pafs our younger yeares,
'tis not likely wee fhould be concern'd
for marrying when old. If wee could
marry now, I don't fee butt thofe in-
conveniencys may happen by ficknefs,
or abfence, or death. In a word, if
we marry, it will be to ferve God and
to encourage one another dayly; if
wee doe not, 'tis for that end too; and
wee know God will direct thofe who
fincerely defire his love above all other
Confiderations; now fhould wee both
refolve to continue as we are, be af-
fur'd, I fhould be as little Idle as if I
were a wife. I fhould attend to prayer
and

and all other Chriſtian dutyes, and
make theſe my pleaſures, ſeeing I chuſe
not the condition out of reſtraint and
ſingularity, but to ſerve God the better."

This being in anſwer to ſomething I
had written to her vpon a ſerious de-
bate, in which I had oppoſed a melancholy Reſolution, ſhe would now and
then entertain me with, of abſolutely
renouncing the thoughts of Marriage
and wholly retireing in the world, I
give you [it] in her owne Style and holy
thoughts, as an Inſtance of that early
piety and prudentiall weighing of things
and circumſtances, which accompanied
all her actions; nor could I have pre-
ſented your Ladyſhipp with a more Illuſtrious part of her hiſtory nor more
inſtructive.

In good earneſt, this purpoſe of
wholly vacateing to Religion, was att
this

this tyme foe imprinted in her, that
whether fhe marryed or remain'd fingle,
refolv'd fhe was to depart the Court.
She had frequently told me, that Seaven
yeares was enough and too much, to
trifle any longer there: and, accordingly, one day that I leaft dream't of it,
fhe came exprefsly to my lodgeing and
accquainted me with her Intention to
goe [and] live att Berkley Houfe, and
that if fhe did alter her condition by
Marriage, it fhould be when fhe was
perfectly free, and had effayed how her
detachment from Royall fervitude would
comport with her before fhe deter-
min'd concerning another change. I
happen'd to be with her in the Queens
withdrawing roome, when a day or two
after, finding her oppertunity, and that
there was lefs company, fhe begg'd
leave of their Majeftyes to retire; never
fhall I forgett the humble and becomeing addrefs fhe made, nor the Joy that
difcover'd its felfe in this Angells countenance

tenance, above any thing I had ever
obferved of tranfport in her, when fhe
had obtained her fuite; for, I muft tell
you, Madam, fhe had made fome at-
tempts before without fuccefs, which
gave her much anxietie. Their Majeftyes were both vnwilling to part with
fuch a Jewell; and I confefs, from that
tyme, I look'd vpon White Hall with
pitty, not to fay Contempt. What will
become faid I, of Corinthus, the Citty
of Luxury, when the graces have abandon'd it, whofe piety and example is
foe highly neceffary? Aftræa foe left
the Lower world. And for my part, I
never fett my foote in it afterwards,
butt as ent'ring into a folitude, and
was ready to cry out with the wife of
Phineas, that its glory was departed.
She tooke, I affure you, her leave of
their Majeftyes with foe much modefty and good a Grace, that tho' they
look't as if they would have a little reproach't her for makeing foe much haft,
they

they could not find in their hearts to
fay an vnkind word to her; butt there
was for all that I am certaine fomething att the heart like griefe; and I
leave you, Madam, to imagine how the
reft of the Court mourn'd this Recefs,
and how dim the tapers burnt as fhe
paff'd the anti-chamber. ' Is Mrs.
Blagge goeing,' fayes a faire creature;
' why ftay I here any longer?' others,
' that the Court had never fuch a Starr
in all its hemifpheere;' and veryly, I
had not obferved foe vniverfall a damp
vpon the fpiritts of every one that knew
her. Itt was, I remember, on a Sunday night, after moft of the company
were departed, that I waited on her
downe to her Chamber, where fhe was
noe fooner enter'd, butt falling on her
knees, fhe bleffed God as for a Signall
deliverance; fhe was come out of Egypt,
and now in the way to the Land of
Promife. You will eafyly figure to
your felfe how buiffy the young Saint
                                    was

was the next morning in makeing vpp
her little carriage to quitt her prifon:
and when you have fancied the Con-
flagration of a certaine Citty the Scripture fpeaks of, imagine this Lady truff-
ing vpp her little fardle, like the two
daughters whom the angell haftned and
conducted; butt the fimilitude goes no
further, for this holy Virgin went to
Zoar, they to the cave of Folly and
Intemperance; there was no danger of
her lookeing back and becomeing a
Statue for forrow of what fhe left behind.   All her houfehold ftuffe befides
a Bible and a bundle of Prayer bookes,
was packed vpp in a very little Com-
pafs, for fhe lived foe farr from fuper-
fluitye, that fhe carryed all that was
vallueable in her perfon; and tho' fhe
had a Courtly wardrobe, fhe affected it
not, becaufe every thing became her
that fhe putt on, and fhe became every
thing was putt vpon her.

She

She tooke her leave of the mother of the Maids as became her; butt fhe could not weepe till your Ladyfhipps fifter, whome fhe was ftill to leave in Captivitye fell on her neck, and then there fell mutuall tears, that trickled downe her Cheeks like the dew of Flowers, and made a lovely griefe: to her and to your Ladyfhipp fhe left her pretty Oratorye, foe often confecrated with her prayers and devotions, as to the only fucceffors of her Virtues and Piety; and as I am perfwaded that the Court was every day lefs fenfible of its loffe whilft you both continued in it, becaufe you trode in this Religious Ladys Stepps, foe the piety it any where ftill retaines is accountable to your rare examples; of fuch Importance is one Religious Perfon to a whole Socie-ty, and fometymes to a Nation.

Butt to returne to her remove from Court. I am the more particular as haveing

haveing had the honour to waite on her to Berkley Houfe; I tell your Lady-fhipp, I never beheld her more orient then fhe appeared att this tyme, and the moment fhe fett foote in the Coach her eyes fparkled with Joy, and a marvelous lufture; the Rofes of her Cheeks were foe frefh, and her countenance foe gay, as if with the reft of her perfections (had fhe not left your two Sifters there) fhe had caryed all the Beautyes as well as all the Virtue of the Court away with her too. Butt ah, had you feen with what effufion and open armes fhe entred Berkley Houfe, and fprung into the Careffes of my Lady, in what a trice after fhe was ledd vp into her apartmentt fhe had putt all her Equipage in order, rang'd her Library, and difpofed of her Compendious Inventory, you would have faid there was nothing prettyer then that buiffy moment. And now when fhe had confecrated her new Oratorye with

with a devout Afpiration and the In-
cenfe of an humble Soule, for the bleffings of this fweete Retirement, fhe
fatt downe and admired her fweet felicitye. For, as I told your Ladyfhipp,
'twas not altogeather that fhe might be
diffengaged from Court that fhe defigned to quitt itt; butt that fhe might
vacate more to ftricter duty. She be-
lieved that att Berkley Houfe fhe fhould
be more att her owne diffpofall; that
fhe fhould have noe body to obferve
butt God; be miftrefs of her houres,
and governe her affaires fuitable to her
devout Inclinations: and when fhe ferioufly requir'd my opinion of it, I
could not diffaprove it. Itt brought to
mind how in the declenfion of the Empire, and when the finns and vices of a
licentious and abandon'd age had al-
larm'd the Roman world with a bar-
barous and vniverfall warr, like what
was now vpon the fcene of Europe,
that Paula and her daughter Euftoch-
ium,

ium, (two rich and beautifull Ladys)
quitted the fplendor of a pompous
Court for the Receffes of Bethelem and
the Solitudes of Judea, and to proftrate
themfelves att the manger of a divine
babe, and then att the foote of Calva-
rye, where this holy Mother and beau-
tious Daughter fpent the reft of their
dayes in the recollection of their lives
and the fervice of Jefus: me-thought nothing more ever refembled this Act of
thofe Devotas than the heroick refolution
of our Saint; in this yett fuperior to
theirs, as hers was fpontaneous, theirs
by the importunityes of St. Hierome;
abandoning the Royall Circle, where fhe
made vp the conftellacions, for a Circle
of reall Starrs, and to ftand before the
throne of the Lamb; fhe deferts the
glittering Balls and goes no more to the
Theater, that fhe may fing in the quire
of Seraphins, and contemplate the celeftiall vifion; fhe cares not for the
Sumptuous Entertainments, the Mu-
fick,

fick, Mafking, and perfumes, to morti-
fye her fences, and enjoy intellectuall
pleafures; fhe neglects the gay and ftu-
dious Drefs, the Raillery and reputation of a Witt, which made her the life
of Converfation and the pretty miracle
of Court, that fhe may adorne her
bright Soule, and converfe with Angells; fhe chufes rather to fuffer diminution, and the cenfure of men as per-
cife and fingular; to be a reall Maid of
Honour, then to have the name, and
live in the fcene of Temptation and
the pleafures of Sinn for a feafon: in a
word, I fancied her call'd, as was Abra-
ham out of Vr of the Chaldees and
from the Idolls of Haran.

Butt as nothing on this fide heaven
is permanent long, fhe had not been in
this Imaginarye and indeed fweete retirement, and where tho' one of the
moft magnificent pallaces of the Towne,
fhe had her apartment remote from the
buifsy

buiffy part of the houfe, and was rarely
fitted for her purpofes of devotion; I
fay, it was not long, when partly from
the neceffity of Complyance with the
Lady of the family, the continuall and
importune vifitts of the great perfons
which vf'd to frequent that place, obligeing her to tedious Cerimony and
converfation that often interrupted her
Courfe, and partly (from) other Circumftances, which for the prefent feemed lefs
favourable to their Intentions of marriage foe foone, and the difquiett it putt
her to, fhe not only deliberated in good
earneft, butt refum'd her former Inclination with more refolution than ever, of
removeing farther from thefe Impediments and all togeather abandoning the
world. I have really been touch'd in the
deepeft fence to fee the Conflicts this devout Creature vnderwent, betweene her
love and her devotion; or fhall I call
them both her love; for foe they were:
a thoufand tymes has fhe told me fhe
would

K

would abide as fhe was, and then her pitty
for him who could not live in her abfence,
divided her afrefh, and peirc'd her to the
foule ; and when fhe was in the deepeft
of this Concerne for him, nothing I
have ever read in the Epiftles of Seneca,
had that excellent Stoick been indeed a
Chriftian, appear'd more divinely philofophicall then the Topics fhe would
vfe to divert his paffion, and reafon
him into an indifference for her, when
(of all things in the world,) it was not
indifferent to her that he fhould have
lov'd her lefs. Butt fhe had really that
abfolute Empire over her owne affections, and fuch potent Inclinations to
make God and Religion the buiffnefs
of her life, that as I faid, fhe was
many times vpon the Brink of Refolve-
ing to abandon all the world : fhe beleived that I who knew love to be
ftronger then death, would never approve of this refolution ; and, therefore, fhe pretended att firft, only to
make

make a vifitt to her fifter the Lady
Yarbrough in Yorkfheir, for a month
or two dureing the fummer; butt after
that, fhe could not conceale from me a
further defigne of goeing from thence
to Hereford, to live by herfelf vnder
the direction of the Reverend Deane of
that Cathedrall, who had long been her
fpirituall father. This was the Zoare
fhe often languifhed after, vfeing that
of Righteous Lott, " Is it not a little
one, and my foule fhall live." "Yes, my
friend," fays fhe, "in perfect libertye
without formes; frugally, without Contempt; conveniently, without pomp;
att diftance from the Buftle of the world,
where I fhall forgett and be forgotten,
be arbitrefs of my tyme, and ferve God
regularly; chufe my Converfation, and
when I alter my Condition, doe it with
your advice; which I am fure will never
be to alter a purpofe foe reafonable, and
foe fitt for one in my Circumftances."
Thus would this bleffed Creature difcourfe

courſe it with me, whilſt in the meane tyme, ſhe was ballanceing in herſelfe when it came to a Reſolution. " The Lord help me, dear freind," ſayes ſhe to me, in another Letter, " I know not what to determine; ſometymes I think one thing, ſometymes another; one day I fancy noe life ſoe pure as the vnmarryed, another day I think it leſs exemplarye, and that the marryed life has more oppertunity of exerciſeing Charity; and then againe, that 'tis full of ſolicitude and worldlyneſs, ſoe as what I ſhall doe, I know not. He can live without a wife willingly, butt without me he. is vnwilling to live, ſoe as if I doe not marry he is not in danger of ſinn; butt if I or he or both ſhould repent, O Lord and Governor of my life, leave me not to my ſelfe, to the Counſell of my whole heart, butt ſend me wiſdome from thy throne to direct, aſſiſt, and lead me ſoberly in my doeings. Thou haſt imparted to us reaſon for

our

our guide; butt O rule thou that reaſon, for without thou Conduct it I ſhall be in perpetuall hazard. Lord, I renounce all Judgment, all knowledge, and diſcretion of my owne; I deſire not to be a Child of this world, wiſe in their Generation, butt to be a Foole that I may indeed be wiſe. I am in a ſtraight and know not what to chuſe, determine thou for me, O bleſſed Lord. Remember that for near theſe one and twenty yeares I have been thy care, and I bleſs the for it. Thou haſt frequently and wonderfully preſerv'd me, both in ſpirituall and temporall dangers, and over and above has done Innumerable good things for me; O leave me not now in this difficulty, butt once more be thou my Councellor, and whilſt I live will I be thy faithfull, thankfull, ſervant. Say, Amen with me, dear freind."

Behold, Madam, the Letter, or rather the ejaculation which an heart intirely

tirely poffeff'd with Religious Senti-
ments, made her dictate on this occafion; nor fhould I have produc'd thefe
particulars (con-credited to me in fpe-
tiall Confidence) butt to lett you fee,
with how holy a defigne and confideracion fhe proceeded; and how Infinitely
different from the method of makeing
love and receiveing addreffes now a
dayes. Veryly, when I reflect vpon her
youth, beauty, witt, the temptations
and conflicts fhe fuftain'd, to comply
with the affection fhe had for her two
Rivall loves (for foe I againe call
them) I am halfe aftonifh'd, butt you
fhall hear how paffionately fhe defcribes
it, and thus goes on.

" Much afflicted and in great agony
was your poor friend this day, to think
of the love of the holy Jefus, and yett
be foe little able to make him any returne. For with what favour have I
protefted againft all affection to the
things

things of this world; refign'd them all without exception; when the firft moment I am tryed, I fhrink away, and am paffionately fond of the Creature, and forgetfull of the Creator. This, when I confider'd, I fell on my knees, and with many teares, begg'd of God to affift me with his Grace, and banifh from me all Concerne butt that of heavenly things, and wholly to poffefs my heart himfelfe; and either releive me in this Conflict, now foe long fuftain'd, or continue to me Strength to refift it, ftill fearing if the combate ceafe not in tyme, I fhould repine for being putt vpon foe hard a dutye. Butt then againe, when I call to mind the Grace of Selfe denyall, the honour of fuffering for my Saviour, the Reward propof'd for thofe that conquer, the delight I fhall conceive in feeing and enjoying him; the happynefs of the life above; I that am thus feeble, thus fearfull, call, (out of exercife of his Grace,) yea, for tribulation,

tion, for perfecution, for contradictions to my owne defires, and for every thing agreeable to the Spiritt and difpleafing to the flefh. Thus, with St. Paul, when I am weake then am I ftrong; when I am in forrow then am I rejoiceing; one whome I love is here, butt I am gott to other Company, and well have I been regal'd, for God has been very gratious to me; moft bitterly have I wept to think how much of my heart he has, how little my bleffed Saviour, who has loved and fuffered for me foe much more; happy, ah happy, are you my friend, that are paft that mighty love to the Creature. Butt I make this my humble confeffion to God and you, bewayleing my loveing any thing butt himfelf; imploreing him to tranflate my affections, and place them on him alone. Thus to you doe I difplay my griefe, I can leave him whome here I love, to goe to my Jefus for ever; butt I Confefs, 'tis hard for me to leave
him

him now foe often as I doe, and this
breaks my heart, that after foe many
folemn profeffions to God, what I would
doe for him, I fhould with fuch reluctancy part from this perfon, to pray,
and to read, and to goe to holy dutyes.

" Now, dear freind, fhould I marry,
and refufe to goe to my Lord, part
vnwillingly, or refufe him, what would
become of me? No, No, I will remaine my Saviours; he fhall be my
love, my hufband, my all; I will keepe
my Virgin, prefent it vnto Chrift, and
not putt myfelfe into the temptation
of loveing any thing in Competition
with my God."

Thus farr this devout and tender
Creature: nor this the laft wherein fhe
has conjur'd me to advife what fhe
fhould refolve on, when often her heart
as I faid, has been divided betweene
her

her lovers, as was St. Pauls in another
cafe, even wifhing to be diffolv'd, that
fhe might be with Chrift, and freed
from all this folicitude, as fhe has frequently expreff'd it to me. And now
what was I to returne? truely I was
myfelfe alfoe fometymes divided in my
thoughts. She had perpetuall Inclinations to retire from all the world, efpetially apprehending that by any fecular
circumftances, fhe might poffibly remaine in a doubtful condition, and the
refolution was once foe ftrongly fix'd,
that with noe fmall dificulty I oppofed
it. Being foe fully perfwaded as I was,
that they would be exceeding bleffings
to one another, rare examples of the
conjugall ftate, and that nothing could
hinder the purfuite of an holy life and
the love of God, foe much as this
pendulous and vncertaine condition,
whilft marriage fhe would find compofe
her devout fpiritt, and improve it, I
told her, fhe was not free, as I con-
ceiv'd,

ceiv'd, to refolve foe peremptorylye;
that it was to doe violence to one
whome fhe acknowledg'd could not live
without her; nay, that if to comply
with her, he putt conftraint vpon himfelfe, fhe fhould not doe well, fince his
Action in this Cafe ought to be as free
as her owne; and that fhe fhould doe a
much nobler and [more] felf denying
thing, to preferr the fatisfaction of foe
worthy a Creature before her owne. I
confented to all her Elogies of the Virgin
State, butt that there were no lefs due
to the Conjugall; and that if there were
fome temptations in it, her meritts would
be the greater, and the exercife of her
virtue; Circled indeed it was with fome
tollerable thornes, butt rewarded with
illuftrious Coronetts for the good it
produc'd; that as to the oppertunityes of
ferveing God, an active life was prefer-
rable to the Contemplative; and that I
fhould not doubt to fee as many Crown'd
in heaven who had been marryed, as of
Virgins:

Virgins: fince from Marriage all the
Virgins in the world had their orriginall,
and all the Saints that ever were or ever
fhall be; that it was the Seminary of
the Church and care of Angells; and
that [though] our beloved [Lord] were
borne of a Virgin, fhe was yett vail'd
vnder the Cover of Marriage; and foe
when St. Paul exalted the Celibate above
it, for the advantages he enumerates,
itt was nott to derogate from Marriage,
butt becaufe of the prefent diftrefs and
the Impediments of a family to an
Itinerant and Perfecuted Apoftle, and
thofe who in that Conjuncture had noe
certaine aboade. That as to the perfection and puritye of the State, 'twas
one thing to be marryed to a Man,
and another to a Hufband; to the firft
indeed, moft of the world were joined,
to the fecond, none butt the Religious.
That as 'twas Inftituted in Paradife,
and dignifyed by our bleffed Saviours
prefence; compared to the moft intimate

mate Indearements of Chrift to his
Church, 'twas often bleffed with exterordinary profperity even in this world.
That the fidelity, fociety, mutuall affection, and inftance of religious Marriages, the regularity of their Charitye,
and hofpitality of their familyes, was
Emulous of the higheft pretences of
the Virgin and more folitary Condition.
Doe you (would I fay) efteeme it noe
honour to have given Saints to the
Church, and vfefull members to the
State in which you live; and that you
can be hofpitable to ftrangers, inftitute
your Children, give inftruction to your
fervants, example to the neighbours,
and be the parent of a thoufand other
bleffings. I remembered her of what
fometymes fhe would fay, that if fhe
marryed and had noe Children, fhe
fhould be difpleafed; and if fhe had,
fhe might have either too many, or too
wicked and vntoward; this, I told her,
was to diftruft Gods providence, and
fhe

fhe did not well to make thofe reflections; when in all events there was ex-
cercife of faith, and patience, Induftry,
and other graces; and that fhe would
not be happy vnlefs fhee was alone, not
confidering that the few may be as well
fooles, as vitious,—which is worfe; and
that one of the many may recompence
all her care for the reft; that if fhe
who bare her had been of that mind,
there would have been one lefs Saint
to Glorifye God; that I fhould have
wanted an excellent friend, and foe
would many others, who now bleff'd
God for the Charityes fhe did them.
Vpon all thefe Topycs I challeng'd her
humility, her faith, and her love. I
laid before her how much more affected,
morofe, covetous, obnoxious to temptation and reproach an old Maid would
be, who was knowne to have engaged
her affection allready, than one who
had never entertain'd an addrefs. Then
the trouble and forrow of bringing
forth

forth and expence of a family, would
att another tyme affreight her; little
weomen, I told her, had little paine;
and that Queens had endured as much
with patience and chearfullnefs; that
as to great fortunes and fupport, opu-
lent couples were not exempted from
Cares, and that tho' I was affured God
had great bleffings of that kind alfoe
in referve; yett fowre provifions and
lefs Ambition, were as happy in the
mutuall affection of each other, where
there was a Competency for the prefent, and foe faire a profpect for the
future: in a word, that there was
fome thing foe patriarchall (not to fay
defpotic) and Royall in a well govern'd
family, and worthy marriages, that I
could not butt give it preheminence to
all fhe had objected. Thefe were the
conflicts wee had on this fubject; and
the difficultyes fhe fuggefted, where, I
plainly told her, Itt was by no means
agreeable to her piety, nor to the Equi-
tye

tye of the thing, that any lefs confideration than a fore fight of inevitable
ruine, fhould fufpend her refolutions of
giveing her felfe to a deferveing perfon
whofe approaches had been foe honourable, and whome fhe confefl'd fhe lov'd
above all the world.   There is certainly
nothing more calamitous, then where
love (as they call it) drives the bar-
gaine, and paffion blinds the Man ; butt
foe the young things precipitate, and
the Giddy are entangled, and when the
fancy cooles, repentance fucceeds, and
it ends in averfion and anxietye.   But
thefe Calentures concern'd not this
excellent Couple, and fuch a Conjuga-
tion of likely circumftances.   I would
tell her itt was not enough to be happy
alone, when fhe might make another
foe ; or ought fhe to refolve not to alter
her Condition till fhe was out of reach
of accidents, that it became a cruell
and ill natur'd Laban to exact a double
apprentyfhipp for a Rachell; that it
                                          was

was Saul that putt David to adventure
for a wife; that the Heroick tymes
were now antiquated, and people proceeded by gentler and more compendious methods; and the decencyes of
her fex, and cuftome of the nation, and
the honour of the condition, and the
want of Monafteryes and pyous Receffes
obliged her to marry. Marry then in
Gods name, faid I, fince my advice you
afke: itt is finally what I think you
ought to refolve on; tho' if I ftuddied
my owne fatisfaction, I fhould rather
promote this averfion, and feeke to fortifye your fufpicion; for as I profefs it
the greateft Contentment of my life
that you have vowed me your friendfhipp foe folemnly, and that you will
be conftant, whilft I incite you to marry,
I endanger and putt it to the hazard;
for perhapps your hufband may be
jealous, tho' without caufe; or he
may have particular diflike to me, or
may not be noble, free, and ingenious,
or

or may make you vnhappy otherwife,
which would be the greateft affliction
could happen to me; whereas, contin-
uing as you are, mifstrefs of your felfe
and your converfation, your virtue and
my yeares, and the confcience of my
duty, and both our difcretions, will preferve our friendfhipp honorable, pious,
and vfefull. In fum, I faid nothing
vpon Marriage, butt what I could vn-
ravell to the advantage of virginitye,—
the eafe of a fingle life, the opportunityes of doeing more good, of ferveing
God better, of prolonging life—by example and precept from Scripture, from
Fathers, from Legends and hiftoryes,
and prefent her fuch a lovely picture
of that ftate, which approaches next
the nature of Angells, (who neither
marry nor are given in marriage) as
would have brought her to more than
a fufpence, or requireing farther advice :
fhe would have needed no farther argument to render her more vnkind to
Hymen,

Hymen, and to the repofe of one who
fhe knew I pittyed; and, therefore, I
ever perfwaded her againft the Recefs
fhe foe often was threatning, as a thing
fingular and of little advantage. I
applauded her recourfe to affiduous and
humble prayer; that God would direct
her for the beft, and that after all I had
faid and written to her, fhe would make
that her Oracle; being confident that
God, who had hitherto taken fuch fignall care of her, would not fuffer her
to mifcarry in this Concerne. For I
could not endure to fee her allwayes in a
doubtfull and vncertaine condition; becaufe it could be profitable for neither,
for when fhe had ferioufly confulted
her friends, fhe had done all that was
required; and fince it could not but
be their vniverfall fuffrage, fhe was to
accquiefs, I therefore advifed her, that
in cafe fhe ftill refolv'd to live as fhe
was, it fhould be butt for a tyme,
without Impofeing on her felfe, and foe
from

from tyme to tyme, as Circumftances might be, butt till then mind her health ; for fhe began to looke pale and leane, and had been too negligent of her felfe, which I reprov'd her for. Butt this did not alltogeather the ef- fect,—fhe rejoines, and writes to me from Twicknam thus :—

"*26th July.*

"Your advice I like, and all you fay on both fubjects ; yett am ftill where I was, wifhing to live alone, as a thing moft fuiteable to my humour, and the neareft way to heaven; nor can you blame one foe weake as I am, to chufe that path which will fooneft bring me to my Journeys end. However, I fhall obferve your Rules, and foe farr your counfell, as not to determine any thing rafhly, till he give me free leave to doe it. In the meane tyme, if you approve of it, that the world may not think by my growing leane as you fay, I

leave

leave it with regrett, for the tyme
I ſtay here, I intend to take care of
my health, and drink the Cows milk
in the Morning, and becauſe I am not
to ſleep imediately vpon it, my Maid
ſhall read to me ſome divine Subject;
then riſe and finiſh my private dutyes,
then pray with my Servants, and be
dreſſed by Eleaven, and ſoe have tyme
before prayers to read a Chapter with
other dutyes; note and collect ſomething out of what I read. Att ſix in
the Evening I will repeate my Courſe
againe, and after that learn ſuch things
by heart as I gladly would retaine;
after Supper pray with my people and
by my ſelfe, my Maid reading to me
whilſt I am vndreſſing, and then lay
me downe in peace. This is the method I intend for ordnary dayes, nott
Frydayes, when you know I am to faſt,
and ſpend it intirely with God; or Sundayes, [when] I will riſe early and Imploy it with as much devotion as I can;
—this

—this is, I fay, the courfe I purpofe here, if you approve of it; for the reft, eat my meate heartyly, and comply with the converfation of the Family; tho' I all this tyme wifh extreamly that I were fetled, where I needed vfe none of thefe Impertinencyes, the obfervances and ceremonyes of vifitts, formall meals, &c. to the expence of my tyme; butt wholly attend on God, night and day. Nor fhould I dare yett to indulge my felfe this liberty, did I att all pleafe my felfe in it as formerly I had done; or that I intend to continue it above 3 months att furtheft, if I change not my Condition, which is to marry (as you would have me) and become worldly. Soe as by the end of Summer, I fhall be free, and then none will confider my lookes, nor fhall I be concern'd if they doe, att the diftance of my retreate. Pray lett me know what you think of all this. I was this day very devout, but nott tender, and I hope it was as well,

well, for I thank God I have made good refolutions."

This being the fubftance of her letter in reply to one of myne, your Ladyfhipp may perceive, as, how devoutly this bleffed Virgin, (for foe muft I call her,) fpent her tyme in that delicious place, and amongft fuch a Confluence of Vifittants, &c, foe how her heart was bent vpon her Northern Recefs, to which I was foe averfe; and I was confident fhe would not long have enjoy'd herfelfe in it; nor could the diftance of Herefordfheir have worne him out of her thoughts, which that of France and Spaine could not doe. The trueth is, I did heartyly pitty that worthy Gentleman, and faw noe reafon in the world why they fhould not both be happy in each other, and my friend compofed, without takeing any exterordnary or fingular courfe; tho' on the other hand, when I confidered thro' what difficultyes

tyes and reluctances, this tender creature, now in the flower of her beauty,
witt, and reputation att court, would
facrifice all to God, I could hardly ab-
ftaine from crying out, O magnanimous
Virgin, I applaud your defigne, I approve, I admire your choice; I mag-
nifye your example; itt is great, 'tis
illuftrious, becaufe it is the better part,
and form'd vpon juft confideration;
you have weighed itt long, and enquired
of God: I allow, I allow, and even en-
vye your purpofe; O fweet repofe of a
devout foule, the flames of Celeftiall
love, the fruition of Jefus, the ante-
pafts of Heaven, what fhall I call, what
fhall I name it; Confumate felicitye
who has none to feare, none to ferve,
none to love butt God; butt whilft you
are made free why leave you me behind, intangl'd in the world, whilft you
are in the light, I [am] in darknefs and a
chaos; for when you are gone what is
the Court or Country to your friend.
I fhall

I fhall fee you no more in the Circle,
nor Joine voices with you in the Quire,
nor vifitt your holy cell; with you our
Joyes are departed, receive me then
from this hatefull abode; and begg
of God, that the circumftances of my
life being compofed, I, who Emulate,
may Imitate your example, and devote
the remainder of my few dayes to eternity; or at leaft while I am to converfe
here below, (for you are gone from
the Earth) may I live in the contemplation of your virtues, and be a part
of your Interceffions. Goe then, my
holy freind, when you pleafe, and be
happy.

Madam, you may poffibly imagine
this a Romantick folly, or the tranfport of fome lover; butt I affure you,
they were the dictates of my mind and
heart, whilft I was Councelling her to
ftay and to marry; for, tho' I thought
this more expedient, I could not but
pronounce

pronounce that the more perfect and exterordnary well. Thus she continued att Twicknam, as it were, in probation, for the most part retired, and sometymes in conversation. He often came to visitt her, and that broke her heart if he abstain'd from comeing. She was still vneasy; soe after some weeks, she returnes to London, with full resolution of beginning her Journey, and the very day was prefixt; butt when it approach'd, indeed it was not possible to pacifye my Lady Berkley; who being to lose the most sweet and agreeable companion in the world, imploy'd all that friendshipp, love, and passion could inspire for the changeing her resolution, and the Convulsion was soe sensible to them both, that she was forced to give way to her Importunityes, and deliberate on it some longer tyme.   Nor was itt alltogeather in the consideration of my Lady alone, that she suffer'd herselfe to be prevailed on, there

there were others whome (when it came
to the Teſt) ſhe was vnwilling to leave
for ſoe long a tyme, and ſoe great a
diſtance, and among them, I ſhould be
ſtrangely vngratefull, not to acknowledge the ſhare I had in her thoughts
and excellent nature, when I ſhall accquaint you of the Reſolution ſhe had
to take a little houſe att Greenwich;
and I had commiſſion from her to find
out a place whither ſhe might retire
to, without quite goeing as it were out
of the world, into the North; not
being able as ſhe affirmed, to comply
any longer with the receiveing and
paying Impertinent viſitts, and other
avocations and circumſtances, which
tooke vpp all her tyme att London, tho'
with a Lady who ſoe much eſteem'd
her. I confeſs, I was not forward to
promote this deſigne, not only becauſe I
thought [it] inconvenient for a Lady ſoe
young, and who was allready diſpoſed
to a more than ordnary reſervedneſs, to
cheriſh

cherifh the humour; butt that it would appeare like fomething over fingular in her and prejudiciall to her health. I propofed therefore, her accepting the beft accomodation I could give her, and fhe had certainly fpent fome confiderable tyme with my wife, and retir'd to the little Cell, where your Ladyfhipp has fometymes found her; butt my Lady Berkley, could not fuffer this Ecclipfe, or endure that fhe fhould goe from her with any patience. Itt was on this that fhe writes me thus at large what conflicts fhe had endur'd; and att the clofe :—" My beft friend as to my being in your family, itt was allmoft, and ah! that it had not been allmoft, butt alltogeather; for whatever you think, it is hard for me to defcribe how forry I am to be thus farr from foe deare a friend; and you don't know that I have given over feverall other propofalls of fettling my felfe, when that thought comes into my head, that I

fhall

fhall be a great way from you, vnlefs I continue where I am att leaft for fome months, till God is pleafed to difpofe of me one way or other."

Butt whilft fhe was in this vncertainty and fufpence where fhe fhould fix, and that the winter began to approach, there was a play to be acted att Court before their Majeftyes, wherein none were to be Actors butt perfons of the moft Illuftrious quality; the Lady Mary, fince Princefs of Orange, the Dutchefs of Monmouth, and all the fhineing beautyes; and itt was not poffible to leave her out, who had vpon the like folemnity formerly, and when fhe was Maid of Honour, accquitted her felfe with foe vniverfall applaufe and admiration; and veryly, never was any thing more charmeing and more a divertifement, than to hear her att any tyme recite, or read a Dramatick poem. She had not only a moft happy memory, butt

butt exquifite Judgment, and could add thofe motions to her voice, as gave what fhe pronounced, the greateft fweetnefs and grace Imaginable. This, tho' fhe would heretofore and butt rarely have done for diverfion, and amongft freinds, the moft innocentt in the world, fhe had now intirely taken leave of, and butt in Complyance with fome great Ladyes (whome fhe could not decently refufe) did fhe willingly fee a play att the Theater; and therefore, to be now herfelfe an Actorefs (tho' among fuch an Affembly of noble Perfons) was to putt a Mortification on her, that coft her not only great reluctancy; butt many teares. Butt there was noe refufeing; the King and Duke had laid their Commands vpon her, to beare a part with the Lady Mary, and others of Illuftrious name. I came often to her when fhe was reciteing, and am wittnefs with what extreame regrett, and how vnwelcome to her this honour

was.

Mrs. Godolphin.

was. Butt fhe had att this moment alfoe anotħer affaire in hand, which more Imported her, and the difficulty in compaffing that which folely by his Majeftes favour was to be obtain'd, dif- pof'd her the more reafonably to com- ply. She had ever fince her Recefs from Court, liv'd in expectation of the pre- fent which of courfe their Majeftyes vfed to make to the Maids of Honour, who haveing waited a competent tyme vpon the Queene, doe either marry or withdraw from Court with their Royall permiffion ; and now had fhe newly folicited the Duke to befpeake my Lord Treafurer about it, who gave her kind words, butt told her he muft have the Kings particular direction in it, butt in the meane while, was not forward to putt his Majeftye in mind of it ; and there was nothing to which fhe had a greater averfion then the Importuneing great perfons in her owne behalfe, for Civility which did not flow naturally

from

from thofe in whofe power it lay to
oblige her. "I perceive," fayes. fhe,
in a letter to me, written 22d September, on this occafion, "that my buiffnefs makes noe advance, and that where
I leaft expected difficulty I find the
greateft. The King fayes nothing to
my Lord Treafurer, nor my Lord to
him; foe that for ought I perceive, 'tis
likely to depend thus a long tyme:
well, Gods will be done, as in Heaven,
foe on Earth; in the meane tyme I am
extreamly heavy, for I would be free
from that place, and have nothing to
doe in itt att all; butt it will not be,
for the play goes on mightyly, which I
hoped would never have proceeded
farther. Dear friend, I begg your
prayers this cloudy Weather, that God
would endow me with patience and
Refignation. Would you beleive itt,
there are fome that envy me the honour
(as they efteeme it) of acting in this
play, and pafs malitious Jefts vpon me.
                                                    Now

Now you know I am to turne the other Cheeke, nor take I notice of itt.

See the humility of this excellent Creature, who you foe well knew, looked on this occafion as one of her greateft afflictions, and would have devolved the fhare fhe had in this Court Magnificence on any other Lady with a thoufand acknowledgments, had their Majeftyes butt excufed her ; butt there was no retreating ; fhe had her part affigned her, which, as itt was the moft illuftrious, foe never was there any perform'd with more grace, and becomeing the folemnity. She had on her that day near twenty thoufand pounds value of Jewells, which were more fett off with her native beauty and lufter then any they contributed of their owne to hers ; in a word, fhe feemed to me a Saint in Glory, abftracting her from the Stage. For I muft tell you, that amidft all this pomp and ferious impertinence, whilft

whilft the reft were acting, and that her
part was fometymes to goe off, as the
fcenes required, into the tireing roome,
where feverall Ladyes her companions
were railing with the Gallants trifleingly
enough till they were called to reenter,
fhe, vnder pretence of conning her next
part, was retired into a Corner, reading
a booke of devotion, without att all
concerning herfelfe or mingling with
the young Company ; as if fhe had no
farther part to act, who was the principall perfon of the Comedy ; nor this
with the leaft difcernable affectation,
butt to divert and take off her thoughts
from the prefent vanity, which from
her foule fhe abhorred.   I mention the
paffage as a fingular work of her reall
piety, and to fhew how fhe continually
applyed her mind on all occafions, and
how little tranfported with thofe fplendid follyes and gay entertainments
which vfually take vp foe much of the
pretious tyme which is given vs to
worke

worke out our Salvation. I need not
enlarge vpon the argument of the
Poem, which you may be fure, however defective in other particulars, was
exactly modeft, and fuiteable to the
Perfons, who were all of the firft rank
and moft illuftrious of the Court : nor
need I recount to your Ladyfhipp with
what a furprizeing and admirable aire
fhe trode the Stage, and performed her
Part, becaufe fhe could doe nothing of
this fort, or any thing elfe fhe vnder-
tooke, indifferently, butt in the higheft
perfection: Butt whilft the whole
Theater were extolling her, fhe was
then in her owne Eyes, not only the
humbleft, butt the moft diffident of
herfelf, and leaft affecting praife.

Thus ended the Play, butt foe did
not her affliction, for a diffafter happened which extreamly concern'd her,
and that was the lofs of a Diamond of
confiderable vallue, which had been
lent

lent her by the Countefs of Suffolke;
the Stage was imediately fwept, and
dilligent fearch made to find it, butt
without fuccefs, foe as probably it had
been taken from her, as fhe was oft in-
viron'd with that infinite Crowd which
tis impoffible to avoid vpon fuch occafion. Butt the lofs was foone repair'd,
for his Royall Highnefs vnderftanding
the trouble fhe was in, generoufely fent
her wherewithall to make my Lady
Suffolke a prefent of foe good a Jewell.
For the reft of that dayes triumph, I
have a particular account ftill by me
of the rich Apparell fhe had on her,
amounting, befides the Pearles and
Pretious Stones, to above three hundred pounds, butt of all which fhe immediately difpofed her felfe, foe foone
as ever fhe could gett clear of the
Stage. Without complimenting any
Creature, or trifling with the reft who
ftaid the collation and refrefhment that
was prepar'd, away fhe flipps like a
Spiritt

Spiritt to Berkley Houſe, and to her
little Oratorye ; whither I waited on
her, and left her on her knees, thank-
ing God that ſhe was delivered from
this vanity, and with her Saviour againe,
never, ſays ſhe, will I come within this
temptation more whilſt I breath.

And thus Mrs. Blagge tooke her
leave of the pomp and glory of the
world, and with freſh reſolutions that
if other circumſtances did not intervene,
namely, ſuch as might ſoe alter her
condition as decently to countenance
her longer ſtay in theſe Parts, ſhe
would yett betake herſelfe to her deſign'd retreat. She was not ſatisfyed
that thoſe who could not butt take notice what Perſon it was ſhe preferr'd
before all the world, ſhould ſpeak of
her withdrawing from Court, and liveing now ſoe long near it without pro-
ceeding any further, tho' divers could
not be driven from the opinion that ſhe

was

was allready marryed. Itt is certaine that excellent Man could never think of parting with her, nor fhe herfelfe from foe many Friends befides, as infinitely vallued her; butt vnlefs he could alfoe decently have taken himfelfe from Court, which was the thing they both projected and defired, that they might wholy quit all dependancys which interrupted their liveing togeather, butt which for many prudent confiderations had been inconvenient for him as yett, fhe was not eafily perfwaded to linger here and be vpon vncertaintyes, who had all along in her Eye the modelling of her life, foe as not to be obliged to thofe complyances fhe was of neceffity to vndergoe in a Station foe near to the Court, vnlefs Mr. G. fhould fix on firme Imployment as might not only countenance her ftay and marrying, butt render other circumftances eafy likewife: tho', as I faid, there was nothing which they

they both did breathe after more then
to have fettled fomewhere remote in
the Country, from all Intanglements of
the World. Thus farr fhe had pleafed
herfelfe to accquaint me with her moft
intimate concerns. I doe not affirme
that to obviate fome objections of hers
he meditated on the purchafe of that
honorable Office which he afterwards
fucceeded in, butt the Mafter of the
Robes, now Earle of Rochefter, dif-
covering his intention about this tyme
to part with that place, might, in my
opinion, be an inducement with them
to marry, and rather truft God with the
event of things, then give the World
occafion, after foe long expectation, to
think fhe made a retreat out of rafhnefs
or difcontent: wherefore vpon the 16th
of May, which was Affention Day,
they both marryed tegeather in the
Temple Church, by the Reverend
Doctor Lake, one of his Royall High-
neffe Chaplaines, my Lady Berkley
and

and a Servant of the Brides onely being prefent, and I think nobody elfe, both the bleffed Paire receiveing the holy Sacrament, and confecrateing the Solemnity with a double Miftery.

Her not acquainting me with this particular of a good while after, occafioned a friendly quarrell betweene vs, that fhe who had intrufted me for many years with all her concerns, nay her greateft Inclinations, and vpon occafion not only named me for the particular Friend that fhould be wittnefs of her Marriage, butt give her to her Hufband, fhould now with fuch Induftry conceale it from me. And now I'le tell your Ladyfhipp how I could not butt difcover it, for noe fooner was the Knott tyed, butt fhe one day defired I would lett her pervfe all the Letters I had of hers, and which fhe knew I too religioufly referv'd, not that fhe could be confcious of haveing ever written
that

that to me which might not have paſt the ſevereſt Eye, butt becauſe there being in many of them profeſſions of the ſinceritye and holy friendſhipp that an excellent Soule (and ſuch as hers was) could expreſs, they might by any accident poſſibly fall into hands that prophane every thing, and moſt, [the] innocent and virtuous ; I failed not to tranſmitt them to her, nor ſhe to re-turne them, as indeed finding nothing in them which ſhould cauſe her to de-prive me of a Treaſure ſhe knew I ſoe in-finitely vallued ; nor could I beleive that tho' ſhe had given [herſelf] to ſoe worthy a Perſon ſhe deſign'd by ſending for her Letters to break with me, as Ladys vſe to doe with vnfortunate Rivalls : for thus ſhe accompanyes her Pacquett :

My Friend, This being Tueſday, a Day which long ſince you know has belonged to a Friend of myne, I have putt togeather all the Letters, Papers, and

and other Fragments, excepting Meditations, which I think you have Coppyes
of, and among which are fome Prayers
of mine, and all your Bookes; only
that you laft fent me, and I am now
reading, of the Intercourfe betweene
Chrift and the Soule, I defire to
retaine, becaufe now and then I am
much pleafed and foftned with fome
paffages of it; and now I have this day
prayed your prayers, thought your
thoughts, wifh'd, I dare fay, your
wifhes, which were that I might every
Day fett loofer and loofer to the things
of this World, difcerning, as every Day
I doe, the folly and vanity of it: how
fhort all its Pleafures, how trifling all
its Recreations, how falfe moft of its
Freindfhipps, how tranfitory every
thing in it, and on the contrary, how
fweete the Service of God, how delightfull the meditateing on his Word,
how pleafant the Converfation of the
Faithfull, and above all, how charmeing

ing Prayer, how glorious our Hopes, how gratious our God is to all his Children, how gentle his Corrections, and how frequently by the firſt Invitations of his Spiritt, he calls vs from our low Deſignes to thoſe great and noble ones of ſerveing him, and attaineing eternall happineſs; theſe have been this Dayes Thoughts and Imployment; for my Lady Hamilton being here, and ſome Freinds att Cards, I have had the whole Day to myſelfe. Rejoyce with me my Friend and be exceeding glad, for ſoe it becomes vs whenever wee have oppertunity of ſerveing him.

And now, Madam, by this, which accompanied the redition of her Letters, your Ladyſhipp may conclude what Courtſhipp there vſed to paſs betweene vs; however, her ſolicitude thus for them on a ſuddaine might well give me vmbrage, and I was reſolved to live vnder an affected Ignorance, aſſured by knowing,

knowing, and as afterwards I learn'd, that this niceneſs could never proceed from herſelfe, but from ſome other prevalent obligation ; and I ever eſteemed it an Impertinence to be over curious, when I found there was deſigne of concealement, and ſhould have much wondred att it of her to me, butt that I was ſoe perfectly accquainted with her Virtues ; whereof one, and that none of the leaſt care in her ſex, was that whenever ſhe was vnder a promiſe of Sacrifice, nothing in the World could vnlock her Boſome, or ſlack her reſolution. A Secrett was indeed a Secrett when comitted to her : and yett againe, when I called to mind the reiterated Promiſſes ſhe had made me never to alter her condition without adviſeing with me, I was ſomtymes in ſuſpence of my Conjectures, and would often reproach myſelfe for the Suggeſtion. Nor did this a little confirme me that ſhe was not marryed, that my

Lady

Lady Berkley now vpon her goeing
with her Hufband, defign'd Ambaſſo-
der Exterordinarye to the Court of
France, and Plenepotentiarye att the
famous Treaty of Nymeghen, ſhe ſo-
lemnly confulted me about her accompanying her Ladyſhipp to Paris, and
ſtaying there with her ſome competent
tyme, to ſee how God would diſpoſe of
things.   I muſt acknowledg I was not
ſoe averſe from this propoſall of hers,
as hopeing it might divert her melancholy defigne and hank[ering] after
Herefordſheir, and ſince my ſon, then
butt a Youth, had importun'd me to
lett him travell, I was the eaſier inclin'd
to gratifye him, vpon the aſſureance I
had of the great care ſhe would have
of him, ſince he was not onely to accompany her in the way, butt be in the ſame
Houſe with her, and in all things in-
join'd to follow her dirrections.   Nor
ever could he have had ſoe bleſſed an
opportunitye of improveing himſelfe ;
this

this little felfe intereft obtain'd on me
I confefs, att that tyme, butt fuch as I
would moft willingly have facrificed,
could I have prevail'd with her to ftay
without purfueing her Notherne Journey, where [the] abandoning herfelfe to
Solitude, muft foone have ruin'd her
health and made her vnhappy.

This excurfion then concluded on,
and lyeing intirely vpon me for her
Provifions and Supplyes abroad, her
mind feem'd to be much att eafe, butt
it was fome Months that this refolution
was taken ere they fett forth, and all
this tyme, I am perfwaded, fhe and her
Hufband liv'd with the fame referves
that the Angells doe in Heaven, not
thinking fitt to cohabitt till they de-
clar'd their Marriage, which for reafons
beft knowne to themfelv's they did
not doe till fhe came back from France
againe.   In this interim, and towards
the latter end of June, fhe did me the
honour

honour to paſs a fortnight att my little
Villa, and brought me a Letter of At-
torney to tranſaɛt all her concerns dureing her abſence, as lookeing now
every Day when my Lord Berkley
would be diſpatched and enter on his
Journey, when behold vpon the 27th
a Fitt of an Appoplexy ſeizing on him
as he was ſitting att the Councell Table
att White Hall, and continueing on
him all that night, without the leaſt
appearance of releaſing him from its
mortall effeɛts, or if that might be poſſible, of ever reſtoreing him to tollerable
ſence and vigour, baniſh'd all thoughts
of Embaſſyes, and conſequently of our
goeing into France. But God was
more gratious to him, for the Phiſitians
had beyond all expeɛtations, and even
amidſt diſpaire, brought him not only
out of this fatall Paroxyſme, butt after
ſome tyme to ſoe much ſtrength (tho'
in moſt men's opinions not perfeɛtly
reſtored to his memorye and abilityes)

as

as nothing would divert him from his intended progreſs. On the 10th of November his Excellency ſett forth with his Traine, my ſon and I accompanying them the firſt Day to Sittinborne; for in regard of his Lordſhipps indiſpoſition they made butt eaſy Journeys. Canterbury was our next nights repoſe; when in the Morning after wee had been att Prayers in the Cathedrall, Mrs. Godolphin and I walking alone togeather, ſhe declared to me what exceeding regrett ſhe was in to leave her Friends. Not without many teares I expoſtulated with her, why ſhe would goe then, I am engaged, ſayes ſhe, to my Lady Berkley, who tells me I breake her Heart if I forſake her, and you ſee in what condition her Lord is, and poore Woman, what would become of her if he ſhould dye, and ſhe have never a Friend by her? nor would I have People think I retire out of any other reſpect. Butt Mr. E. if ever I returne

returne againe, and doe not marry, I will ftill retire, and end my Dayes among you, and you are like to have the fhare of the trouble: for fhe had often faid fhe would divide her Life among her Freinds, and did me the honour to putt me into the Rank of one of the firft.

This, Madam, was the only tyme that in her Life fhe ever prevaricated with me, and cover'd it with that ad-drefs; and was, I am moft affured, in deepeft forrow, as all my former fufpi-cions of her being marryed vanifh't. Doe you not think, fayes fhe, that it afflicts me to the Soule to part with you, and from one who I am fure you beleive I love intirely, and leave in my Condition? This, vttered with a fflood of forrow, I was not able to fuftaine without reciprocall kindnefs and ten-dernefs. Butt the tyme now call'd us to break off this Converfation, the fad-deft

deft that in my Life I ever faw [her] in;
fhe had left her Heart att another Place,
and with one that therefore did not accompany her, becaufe he was of a tender nature, and durft not truft his Paffion, whilft their Defigne was to conceale their relation. Wee arrived this
evening att Dover, where, after Supper,
calling me into her Chamber, fhe fign'd
and delivered me her Will, before her
Maid, wherein fhe had me her Ad-
miniftrator; for it feemes her Hufband
had impower'd her to difpofe of what
fhe pleaf'd, and as fhe pleafed, as afterwards fhe told me: this done, fhe defir'd I would pray with her, and foe I
left her, as full of Sorrow as fhe could
hold.

Early the next Morning I waited on
her againe, and againe, and fell into the
fame refentments; and that now fhe
was foe near the tyme when fhe muft
be feparated from them fhe lov'd, I
know

know not how, faid I, you part from
your Lover, butt never may you feele
what it is to part from a Friend. I
beleive there is one that you really love,
and that 'tis mutuall, how is it then
you thus goe from him, and he from
you? this is ftrange proceedings, 'tis
fpirituall, 'tis high, 'tis myfterious and
fingular; but find it a name if you can,
for I confefs I vnderftand it not: doe
you preferve ferenity of mind, and yett
continue languifhing? Nothing is in
nature foe repugnant as Love and abfence, where nothing forbidds the object
to be prefent. O heroick Soules, if
you think to be att eafe, I fhall be
glad; butt greatly oblig'd to learne the
Secrett, and be taught to beare this
Divulfion with as little paine, fince I
know of noe Ingagement you have to
goe from your Friends and thofe whome
you profefs to love. Goe back, goe
back then, and be happy both, for this
Courfe will weare you both out, if
really

really you love him. For goodnefs
fake doe not break my Heart (fays
fhe), you fee I am engaged; and then
fhe wept and wore fuch a cloud of Sorrow all that Morning, that fhe could
hardly fpeake a word when I lead her
downe to the Company, now prepareing to goe on board. Itt was vpon
the 13 of November that vpon the
Beach wee tooke folemn leave, and I
fhould difcover too much of my weak-
nefs to exprefs the trouble I was in, to
fee her overwhelm'd with grief that fhe
could not fpeake one word; butt thus
fhe was carried into the Yatch, when
being a little launched into the Sea, the
Fort from the Caftle gave his Excel-
lencye 17 Guns, and was anfwered with
five, according to the Forme.

I recount this paffage to your Ladyfhipp more minuitely, as being the
moft paffionate and moft myfterious;
nor will I therefore make any reflections

tions on it then what I am perfwaded
your Ladyfhipp muft doe, and then
conclude them with admiration how
two Perfons that lov'd each other foe
intirely, could fupport a Divorce foe
long; or what might be the Caufe, if
any other there were, butt a fingular
and extreame nicenefs not to come togeather, which they might be fufpected
to doe, however to appearance they
lived referv'd, till they publickly avow'd
their Marriage, which you may remember they forbare till they had made
their Familyes and Equipage com-
pleate.

On the 5th of December, fhe writt
me word of their fafe arrivall att Paris,
and how they had difpof'd of them-
felvs; togeather with an Account of
my Lord Ambaffadors magnificent En-
try and Audience att the French Court,
with other pompious Circumftances,
which yett foe little concern'd this admirable

mirable Creature, that fhe would onely
be noe Spectator of it, butt not foe
much as once appeared att Court all
the tyme of her being att the Ambaffadors Houfe. And tho' the Report
of fuch a Beauty and Witt had foe
forerun her arivall, by fome who had
known her in the Circle att Court, that
the French King was defireous to fee
her in that att Saint Germans; yett fhe
foe order'd matters as to avoid all occafions of goeing thither, and came
back to England without giveing that
great Monarch the fatisfaction of one
Glaunce, or her felfe of the Splendor
or Vanity of his Court; which is foe
fingular a Note in her fex, and of one
naturally foe curious and obferveing,
that I cannot pafs it over without a
juft remarke, efpecially being a Lady
foe infinitely compleafant, and of a nature foe obligeing, Miftrefs alfoe of the
French Tongue to fuch perfection, as
rendered her capable of entertaining

Perfons

Perſons of the higheſt qualitye, nor was this reſervdneſs out of humour or ſingularity. She now conſiders her ſelfe a marryed Woman, and tho' ſhe went over to accompany my Lady, there was no neceſſity for her to appeare att Court, where the virtues of ſtrangers did not allwayes protect the Sex from Inconveniencyes; and ſhe was reſolv'd to give no occaſion to be talk'd of or admir'd. All the Tyme ſhe could redeeme from thoſe Civilityes ſhe owed my Lady, and which now begun to be very tedious to one whoſe Heart was in another Country, ſhe ſpent in Devotion, reading excellent Bookes, and converſeing with ſome few of her Accquaintance, butt without gratifyeing her curioſity by goeing out to ſee the many rarityes which the famous Citty ſhe was in invites all ſtrangers to, vnleſs it were that of her goeing one afternoone to a Cloyſter of Nuns; whoſe manner of liveing did not diſpleaſe

pleafe her, whilft nothing of their Superftition could endanger one foe well
principled in her Religion. I will give
your Ladyfhipp a tranfcript of the firft
Letter fent me after her arrivall att
Paris, to confirme it.

" My Friend, I promifed you an Account of our Journey hither; there was
nothing in it of exterordnary, no ill accident, nothing like Pintos Travells. Since
I came to Paris, I have hardly been out
of doores to vifit any body, butt there
has been a Preift to vifitt me; butt
without Vanity I think I faid as much
for my Opinion as he did for his. I
am now reading Mounfieur Clauds
Defence de la Reformation, and like it
moft exceedingly; foe as you need
have noe fear of me on that fide. God
knows, the more one fees of their
Church, the more one finds to diflike
in itt; I did not imagine the tenth
part of the Superftition I find in it, yett
ftill

ftill could approve of their Orders. Their Nunneryes feem to be holy Inftitutions, if they are abufed 'tis not their fault: what is not perverted? Marriage itt felfe is become a fnare, and People feem to difpofe of their Children young, left the remedy increafe the diffeafe: butt when I have commended that baile of theirs, I have faid for them, I think, all that reafonably can be faid. One thing I muft tell you, Friend, People can have the Spleens here in Paris, lett them fay what they will of the Aire; butt if Arithmetick will cure itt, I am goeing with my Charge, your Son, to be a very hard Student, and wee intend to be very wife."

I prefent you, Madam, with this Fragment of a Letter, to fhew your Ladyfhipp how fhe fpent her Tyme, when fhe could redeeme it from Complyances with the Company, and the Decencyes

Decencyes of fuch Vifitts as were not
to be refifted where Perfons of Qualitye came to fee her; butt of which fhe
grew foe weary att laft—and for another
reafon you may conjecture,—as within
a Month or two of her arrivall, this
excellent Creature was quite fick of
France.

" I am weary," fays fhe, in another
Letter to me of the 4th of February,
" of my Life, I have here no tyme for
my Soule. Cards wee play att four
Houres every Day; whoever comes to
vifitt, I muft be by to interprett; where
ever a certaine Lady goes (if my Lady
H. be not att hand), I muft trudge;
foe that poore I can fcarce fay my
Prayers, and feldome or never read.
Dear Friend, pray heartyly, that if it
be Gods will, I may be reftor'd to my
owne People, and to my God; for
tho' he be every where I cannott call
vpon him as I was wont att home:
therefore

therefore for God's fake pray that I may fpeedily and once againe worfhipp him in his Congregation, and enjoy the affiftance of his Grace, the prefence of my beft Freinds, whom as my Life I love. I could content my felfe with any thing, I think, were I once att home. Butt I muft doe nothing rafhly; I hope yett in God through your Prayers, and my owne firme Refolutions, to gett home affoone as ever I can, being quite wearyed with dedicateing my felfe perpetually to other People. 'Tis almoft one a Clock ere I can gett to Bedd, foe that in the Morning I am not able to rife before Eight, and paffing then an Hour in Prayer and Pfalmes, and an Houre and a halfe in reading, fometymes one Booke, fometymes another, by the tyme I am dreff'd Publique Prayers begin; then follows Dinner, then Talk till 3, then goe to Publick Prayers, then prate againe, God knows till Six a Clock,

a Clock, and then with much difficulty
gett away to pray, for my felf, for
you, and fome other, then am I call'd
to Cards till Bed tyme. O pittye, pittye me, dear Friend!"

I fhall need repeate noe more of her
fad laments; diverfe have I by me, and
yet it was ftill more for this interrup-
tion of her affiduous courfe and devotion than for any other confideration.
She lookes vpon it as an Exile from
the Houfe of God, which like holy
David, was to her intollerable. Even
amongft the circumftances of fplendor,
eafe, and worldly diverfion, fhe had
been made beleive fhe fhould be as
much Miftrefs of her retirements att
Paris as fhe was wont to be att Berkley
Houfe: tho' neither there was fhe att
the Liberty fhe breath'd after, Devotion, and Solitude, and Leafure for the
improvement of her Mind. Butt this
Affliction did not laft, for vpon my
Lord

Lord Ambaſſadors prepareing to goe to Nimoghen, and a reall pretence of an Affaire that concern'd her, namely, the diſpoſeing of a conſiderable ſumme of mony intruſted with me, ſhe decently tooke the oppertunitye of Mr. Bernard Greenvile returneing out of Italy, (whither he had been ſent with a Publique Character to the great Duke of Tuſcany) and paſſing through Paris, of being conducted by that honorable and worthy Gentleman, without thoſe difficultyes ſhe might otherwiſe have mett with : nor doubt I butt my Lady Berkley, who was privy to her being marryed, and had now another Lady with her, leſs ſcrupulous and more diverting, was the eaſier wrought on to part with one ſhe could ſuffer to be ſupplanted by another, after ſuch profeſſions of the moſt ſuperlative Friendſhipp and Indearments in the World, and which, I am certaine, contributed not a little to what afflicted this tender and good natured Creature.

Mrs.

Mrs. Godolphin (for foe now I call her) haveing thus taken leave of Paris, arrived att Dover the 3d of Aprill, in which interim I had by her direction order'd her Accomodations to be remov'd from Berkley Houfe to Doctor Warnetts in Covent Garden, whofe wife was her near relation. Soe on the Sixth of Aprill fhe gave me notice of her being come to London, where the next Day I waited on her, to the no fmall Joy, you may be fure, of all her Friends, as well as of my felfe. I will not repeate to your Ladyfhipp what had allready paff'd betweene vs in freindly expoftulations, for the vnkind-nefs of her foe long concealing from me the circumftance of her Marriage, becaufe fhe had expreff'd her Sorrow with fuch an affeveration as in my whole Life before I never heard her vtter, foe as I could not butt forgive her heartyly.   Nor did this fuffice, for
fhe

she often acknowledg'd her fault, and
beg'd of me that I would not diminish
ought of my good Opinion of her, to
the least wounding the intire Freind-
shipp which was betweene vs; protest-
ing she had been soe afflicted in her
selfe for it, that were it to doe againe,
noe consideration or complyance in the
World should have prevailed on her to
break her Promise, as some had done
to her regrett. In good earnest I was
sorry to see her troubled for it, con-
sidering the Empire of a passionate
Love, the singular and silent way of
the Lover, whose gravitye and temper you know soe well, and with whome
I had nothing of that intimacy and in-
dear'd Friendshipp, which might intitle
me to the Confidence he has since
not thought me vnworthy of. I therefore mention this passage, becaufe she
was a Person of soe exact and nice
a Conscience, that for all the World
she would not have violated her Promise;

mife; nor did I ever find it in the leaft fave this, which, when all is done, was of noe great importance.   Save that I tooke it a little to heart fhe fhould foe induftrioufly conceale a thing from one to whome fhe had all along comunicated her moft intimate thoughts; and when that affection of hers was placed, which fhe would often acknowledge was not poffible for her to moderate as fhe defir'd, or bring to the leaft indifference, after all her innocent ftratagems and endeavours, and even fometymes refolutions, to quitt all the World, and think of him only in her Prayers.

This fcene being thus over, to my great fatisfaction, and, as vpon all occafions I advifed, when thofe melancholy thoughts and fancyes vf'd to interrupt her quiett, wee will looke vpon this Lady now, as a fetled Woman, and in the Armes of that excellent Perfon the moft worthy to poffefs her.   Itt
was

was on the 13th of Aprill that fhe did
me the honour of a vifitt att my houfe,
exprefling infinite acknowledgments to
Almighty God for his goodnefs to her,
after a moft folemn manner, and that
once againe fhe was come among her
friends, beging of me, that I would
continue to affift her with thofe little fervices fhe was pleafed to accept.   And
now haveing thought fitt to make their
marriage noe longer a fecrett,—for fhe
had not yett, I think, revealed it to her
fifter, nor did his Majeftye or Court,
know any thing of it, till fhe was in
Equipage to appeare as became her—
fhe obtained of the Queen a confiderable augmentation of a Leafe fhe had
of certaine Lands in Spalding, about
which fhe was pleafed to make vfe of
my affiftance, for the fettlement of it.
This was in May, and by the next month
fhe had furnifh'd and formed her pretty
family att Berkley houfe, whether on
the 27th of June, fhe removed out of
Covent

Covent Garden, and began to receive
the vifitts and vfuall Congratulations
vpon Marriages, foe vniverfally ap-
proved of.

Dureing this, I had the good fortune
to fecure a confiderable fumme due to
her, which lay in fome danger. V. in
September began to build and accomodate that pretty habitation for her in
Scotland yard, which fhe contrived and
adorn'd with foe much Ingenuity and
decency; and where your Ladyfhipp and
all who knew and lov'd that excellent
creature, have been foe chearfull, foe
happy, and foe vnhappy, that I never
can pafs or think vpon the place butt
a thoufand fad thoughts affect me.

Itt was dureing the fitting of that
Lodging, that fhe came downe to vs
att Sayes Court againe, and bleffed the
little appartment you know, with her
prefence, from the 28th of September,

to

to the 19th of October, her hufband then being att Newmarkett with his Majefty; nor can your Ladyfhipp forgett how fweetly fhe liv'd in their retirement all this winter, till hearing of my Lord Berkleys returne from his Embaffey, fhe thought fitt to remove to her owne Lodgings, now finifhed att Whitehall for alltogeather; which accordingly fhe did on the laft of March, fettling with that pretty and difcreete oeconomye foe naturall to her; and never was there fuch an houfehold of faith, never Lady more worthy of the bleffings fhe was entering into, who was foe thankfull to God for them.

"Lord," (fays fhe, in a Letter to me) "when I this day confidered my happynefs, in haveing foe perfect health of body, chearfullnefs of mind, noe difturbance from without, nor griefe within, my tyme my owne, my houfe quiett fweete and pretty, all manner of Conveniencys

veniencys for ſerveing God, in publick
and private, how happy in my Friends,
Huſband, Relations, Servants, Creditt,
and none to waite or attend on, but my
dear and beloved God, from whome I
receive all this, what a melting joy run
through me att the thoughts of all theſe
mercyes, and how did I think myſelfe
obliged to goe to the foote of my Redeemer, and acknowledge my owne
vnworthineſs of his favour : butt then
what words was I to make vſe of; truely att firſt of none att all, but a devout
ſilence did ſpeake for me ; but after that
I power'd out my prayers, and was in
an amazement that there ſhould be ſuch
a ſin as ingratitude, in the world, and
that any ſhould neglect this great duty ;
butt why doe I ſay all this to you my
friend ? truely that out of the abundance of the heart, the mouth ſpeaketh,
and I am ſtill ſoe full of it, that I cannot forbeare expreſſing my thoughts to
you."

And

And that this was not a tranfient rapture, vpon the fence of her prefent Enjoyment, butt a permanent and devout affection; vpon the 16th day of October following, which day fhe conftantly vfed to give me an account of her concernes the year paft, I find this paffage in a Letter.

" God Allmighty has been Infinitely gratious to me this year, for he has brought me back into my owne native Country in fafety, and honourably profpered me in my temporall affaires; above my expectation continued my health, and my friends; deliver'd me from the torments of fufpence; given me a hufband that above all men living I vallue; in a word, I have little to wifh butt a Child, and to contribute fomething to my friends happynefs, which I moft impatiently defire; and then I muft think before I can remember,

ber, what I would have more then I
enjoy in this world, butt the continuance of a thankfull heart to my God."

This, Madam, was the vſe and the
gratefull returne ſhe made of the ſhort
bleſſings ſhe enjoyed. Nor need I accquaint your Ladyſhipp, with what care
ſhe inſtructed her ſervants, how ſedu-
louſly ſhe kept her family to Religious
dutyes, how decently ſhe received her
friends, how profitably ſhe imployed
every moment of tyme. Nothing in this
world had ſhe more to wiſh, butt what
God ſoone after gave her, that ſhe
might be Mother of a Child ; which
ſhe ſoe paſſionately deſir'd after two
yeares that ſhe yett had none, as in
the intervall ſhe tooke home to her, a
poore orphan girle, whome ſhe tended, inſtructed and cheriſhed, with the
tenderneſs of a naturall mother. For I
have beheld when ſhe dreſſ'd and vn-
dreſſ'd it, and laid it to ſleep with all
the

the circumftances of a carefull Mother
and nurfe; till it pleafed God to give
her certaine hopes of the blefling fhe
thought onely wanting to confumate
her happynefs. Nor did (as your Ladyfhipp well knows) any Inconveniency
of that burthen, att all flacken her devout courfe, but improve it rather;
when to other confiderable Charityes a
little before fhe was brought to bedd, fhe
fent me £.70 to diftribute; by which
were releived many indigent people and
poore houfe keepers; and this was her
owne entirely, for her excellent hufband
had the year before fetled on her, not
onely the product, but abfolute difpofall
of the portion which fhe brought, to
above £.4000, for the irreverfible continuance thereof, they were pleafed to
intruft me to manage the Stock, foe as
now haveing ftill wherewithall to in-
large her Charitye, without prejudice;
there was indeed nothing wanting which
fhe defired more in the world, as often
fhe

fhe would repeate it to me, butt the life
of that Dear Man, for foe fhe called her
hufband, for whome fhe had now and
then much apprehenfion, fubject as he
was to fevors that had formerly en-
dangered him, not in the leaft fore-
bodeing of her owne departure, and
leaveing him behind her; tho' vpon a
dreame of myne I once related to her
fome yeares before, fhe affirmed with
much earneftnefs that fhe fhould certainely dye before me : which tho' I
tooke little notice of then, and beleived
nothing lefs, I cannot butt fince reflect
vpon; efpecially when I call to mind,
the order fhe gave the painter, that in
the picture fhe fome years fince beftowed vpon me, fhe would be drawne
in a lugubrous pofture, fitting vpon a
Tomb ftone adorned with a Sepulcher
Vrne ; nor was this att all my fancy, butt
her exprefs defire. Butt to lay noe more
ftrefs on this, how frequently have I
heard her fay, fhe loved to be in the
houfe

houfe of Mourning. Nor does your Ladyfhipp forgett how a few dayes before her Reckoning was out, my Lady Vifcountefs Mordant giveing her a vifitt, and finding her Eyes fwollen with teares, fhe told her fhe had being doeing a fad, yett to her a pleafing thing, and that was the writeing fomething to her hufband which fhe requefted he would doe for her, if fhe fhould dye of that Child; and then added the great Comfort and fatisfaction it was to her, that fhe had putt her little concerns in order, and otherwife made preparations againft all furprizes, and was perfectly refign'd. This difcourfe for the prefent drew mutuall Tears, butt abated nothing of her wonted chearfullnefs: when on the fifteenth of May, which was the Anniverfary of her marriage, fhe with your Ladyfhipp and fifter Gr. honour'd my poore houfe with a vifitt, (the laft fhe ever gave me, and therefore not to be forgotten) the perfect good humour fhe

ſhe then was in renders the memory
of it ſad, as well as that ſhe was in the
July after, when wee all went with her
to Mr. Aſhmoles att Lambath who diverted her with many curioſityes : butt
after this, growing bigger ſhe rarely
ſtirr'd abroad, ſave to the Chappell. Itt
was yett againe on the fourth of Auguſt,
that my Lady Mordant and my wife
(by aſſignation betweene them) went to
dyne with her att her pretty appartment,
they found her well, butt ſomething
more then vſually ſolemne ; ſhe had it
ſeemes been reading and ſorting of papers and Letters, and how, ſayes ſhe, is it
poſſible to think of ones friends wee are
to leave behind, without concernment ;
with diſcourſe to this purpoſe. This
more then ordinary Impulſe, that ſhe
ſhould not outlive the happineſs ſhe had
ſoe long wiſhed for, made the Converſation leſs gay and chearfull then otherwiſe it was wont to be, and it ſeemes to
me, ſhe had ſome apprehenſions exterordinary,

ordinary, which were not difcern'd by any of her friends; when often wifhing that fhe might, if foe it pleaf'd God, bring her hufband one Child, and leave him that pledge of her intire affeċtion. She feemed to thirft after nothing more than to be with God; and veryly what eftimate fhe tooke of thefe poore fatis-faċtions here, when I have fometymes refleċted on the circumftances of her youth and chearful temper, with the profpeċt of as much worldly happynefs as fhe could defire, I have extreamly wonder'd att her contempt of it, finding likewife that it did not proceed from any peevifh difcontent or fingularitye of humour, butt from a philofophicall, wife and pious confideration of the viciffitude and inftabilitye of all earthly fruitions, and an ardent longing after that glori-ous ftate, where (faid fhe) I fhall be perfeċtly att repofe, and fin no more. And that thefe were allmoft her contin-uall thoughts and afpirations, fee how
fhe

fhe entertaines me, in a poftcript about the very tyme.

" Lett vs pray, that Gods Kingdome of Grace being received into our hearts, his Kingdome of Glory may fucceed, and foe wee ever be with the Lord; which indeed I long for, more then all the fatisfactions of this world; really Friend there's nothing in it to be chofen for itfelfe. Is not eating to fatisfye the paine of hunger, fleepe to eafe our wearynefs, and other divertifements to take off the mind from being too intent on things that it cannot allwayes fupport without great inconveniency to its facul-tyes? Retirement againe is to difcharge it of that burthen, and the ftaines it has contracted by being in converfation, and impertinent Company; foe that vpon the matter, our intire life is in my opinion, an inquiry after remedyes, which doe often if not allways exchange rather than cure our infirmityes; I ac-knowledge

knowledge that God has imparted to me
many great bleſſings, which if our nature were not fadly deprav'd, wee might
exceedingly rejoyce in, butt wee make
foe ill vfe of moſt of them, that wee
turne thofe things to mifcheifes, which
are given to vs for our good &c." In this
ſtyle fhe goes on, and could a Seneca,
or an Antoninus, or indeed the wifeſt
and holyeſt perfon have vttered [aught]
more divine and piouſly ferious : nor
did fhe fay this only, butt fhe practiſ'd
it : for with what devout and folemne
preparations paſſ'd the reſt of this fatall
month ! Haveing received the bleſſed
facrament butt two dayes before fhe
was brought to bedd, foe preventing
all poſſible furprizes, and waiteing now
with her wonted alacritye and refignation the approach of the conflict fhe
was to enter vpon, fhe on the fecond of
September, began firſt to be fenfible of
fome alteration in her temper, and dureing that night it was concluded it might
be

be her labour, and foe it was. With what exceeding patience, devotion, and courage fhe fuftain'd it, your Lady-fhipp, who was all the tyme affifting, with both thofe excellent fifters, can beft tell.

Itt was then on Tuefday the third of that vnfortunate Month, when come-ing about 11 a clock in the forenoone as my cuftome was, to vifitt her and afk of her health, that I found fhe was in Travell; and you may eafyly imagine how extreamly I was concern'd, not to ftirr from the houfe till I had fome af-fureance that all fucceeded well. And indeed to all appearance foe it did. For it pleaf'd God that within an hour, your Ladyfhipp brought me the joyfull ty-deings of a Man Child born into the world, and a very little after admitted me to fee and blefs that lovely Babe by the Mothers fide; when the very firft word fhe fpake to me was, I hope you

have

have given thanks to God for his infinite mercy to me; O with what satisfaction, with what joy and over rapture did I hear her pronounce it, with what satisfaction and pleasure, did I see the Mother safe, and her desire accomplished, without any accident that could give the least vmbrage or suspicion of approaching danger, soe as me thought of nothing more then rejoyceing and praiseing God, augureing a thousand benedictions.

In this faire and hopefull condition she continued all that day, when her husband, now att Windsor with the Court, being sent for to come to double and compleat the Joy, upon the Thursday following, his little Son was made a Christian, [his name Francis] in presence of both the parents; his Vnkle Sir William Godolphyn, Mr. Harvey, Treasurer to her Majestye, and Lady Berkley being susceptors; the Chaplaines
who

who conftantly vfed to fay prayers in the family, performeing the office.

Seeing this dear Lady foe well layd, the Child Baptized, and every thing in a hopefull way, my wife, who was now to vifitt her, and I, return'd home, as full of joy and fatisfaction as wee could be, for the beft and moft eftimable friend wee had in the world; butt ah, how were wee both furprized, when on the Sunday following there was a Letter delivered me in the Church, about the latter end of the Morning Sermon, in this dolefull ftyle.

" My poore wife is fallen very ill of a ffevor, with lightnefs in her head. You know who fayes the prayer of the faithfull fhall fave the fick; I humbly begg your charitable prayers, for this poore creature and your diftracted fervant. London: Saturday, 9 a clock."

O how

O how was I ftruck through, as with a dart. I am not able to tell your Ladyfhipp with how fad and apprehenfive thoughts my wife and I haftned imediately to Whitehall; where wee found her in all the circumftances of danger; and tho' diftinctly knowing thofe who came to vifitt and were about her, yett had the diftemper allready foe farr prevailed on her fpiritts, that it was a fad and mournfull thing to find how her fancy and vfuall temper was diforder'd. To all this, the feafon happen'd to prove exceffively hott, which exceedingly contributed to her fuffering. There had been, when I came, butt one phyfitian fent for; butt my wife, fufpecting (with others) that this violent furprize could not likely proceed from either the intemperance of the weather or impaire of one, foe well laid as to all appearance as fhe was, butt poffibly from accident, itt was thought advifable to call an experienc'd

enc'd perfon in cafes of this nature.
Butt itt was fo very long ere the doctor
could be found, and foe late ere he
came, that through the frequency and
violence of her fitts, which were now
delirious, her fpiritts were foe farr
wafted, that tho' he were of the fame
opinion, and that fomething was omitted, yett would he by no intreaty be
perfwaded to apply any thing butt in
conjunction with other phifityans. Doctor Lowther being call'd away fome
houres before, and befides it being now
farr in the night, itt was with exterordinary dificulty that I gott my antient
dear and religious friend, Doctor Needham, fince with God, and then but
valetudinarye himfelfe, to come. Others
who were fent for, wearyed as they pretended with toyle, would not be prevailed with to rife, except Doctor Short;
foe as till now, there had been little attempted ; nor any thing even by thefe
with any affureance, foe farr fhe was
                                    fpent

ſpent, and her condition not admitting
of proper remedyes for what they
feared, gave ſlender hopes of ſucceſs.
The Deliriums increaſe, and allbeit
with ſome promiſe and intermiſſions, to
appearance, yett were they only ſuch
as proceeded from languor and tired-
neſs; ſoe that tho' ſhe ſtill retained her
memory of the perſons about her, what
ſhe ſaid was altogeather inconſiſtent,
and growing more impetuous and de-
plorable, gave preſage of uttmoſt danger. This only was highly remarkeable,
that in all this diſorder of fancy and
allmoſt diſtraction, ſhe vttered not one
ſyllable or expreſſion that might in the
leaſt offend God, or any creature about
her; a thing which dureing theſe alien-
ations of mind does ſeldome happen;
butt which ſhewed how bleſſed a thing
it was to live holylye and carefully, as
this Innocent did; perſons that are delirious vſually vttering extravigancyes
that diſcover their worſt inclinations.

Butt

Butt fhe was now in a manner fpent,
and no't could phyfitians doe, when
neither the cupping nor the pidgeons,
thofe laft of remedyes, wrought any
effect. Other things had been perhapps convenient ; butt there was noe
ftrength to bear inward remedyes, when
even the moft gentle had been fatall ;
and there now appearing a kind of
Erifypulus on her back, neck, and armes,
the malignancy grew defperate,—and
this excellent Creature paffes a fiery
Triall, exercifed in all the circumftances
of paine and wearynefs. Wee beheld
her now languifhing vnder the laft conflicts till the morning of the next day.
There had been, your Ladyfhipp
knows, a confultation the night before,
and a refolution of attempting fearch-
ing att a venture, if fhe lived till day,
and the rather that the phyfitians might
not feeme to doe nothing in a defperate
cafe, than expecting any good effect
without a miracle. Butt when the morning

ing came, finding her ftill more debili-
tated, and the paroxyfmes impetuous
and allmoft vnceffant, all hopes being
given over, vpon the importunitye and
recomendation of that excellent and
pious lady, the Vifcountefs Mordant,
they permitted one Doctor Ffaber to
make tryall of a Cordiall, celebrated by
her Ladyfhipp for the great matter it
had performed, and indeed it feem'd
att firft to compofe her, and fomewhat
allay the violence of her fitts. Butt the
moments were fhort, and her conflict is
repeated, with the vfuall violence; till
fhe who was wont to raife her felfe vp
as oft as they came, now finkes downe
as no more able to fuftaine them; her
fpiritts faint: till no more pulfe per-
ceiveable,—for your Ladyfhipp and I
held her all this while by the hands,—
with the moft ardent prayers and offices
of the holy Man, who continually attended, he earneftly, and wee all devoutly recomend, and fhe quietly renders

ders vp her happy foule to her bleffed Redeemer, in whofe bofome fhe is now deliver'd from all earthly mifferyes, and affumed into thofe blifsfull Manfions prepared for his Saints, and fuch as like her excellent in virtue.

Thus ended this incomparable Lady : our never to be fufficiently lamented loffe : leaveing not onely a difconfolate Hufband, whofe vnexpreffible griefe and deep afflidtion would hardly fuffer him to be fpedtator of her languifh- ments, drown'd in tears and proftrate att the mercy feate, butt all her Re- lations, and who had the honour to know her in as much reall and pun- gent forrow as Chriftians and tender hearts were capable to exprefs, and as was highly due for foe fencible and vni- verfall a lofs, and foe infinitely de- plor'd.

This fatall houre was (your Ladyfhipp

shipp knows) about one o'clock, att noone on the Munday, September the nineth, 1678, in the 25 year and prime of her age. O vnparalell'd lofs! O griefe indicible! By me never to be forgotten—never to be overcome! Nor pafs I the fad anniverfary and lugu-bruous period, without the moft fenci-ble emotions, forrow that draws tears from my very heart whilft I am recite-ing it.

Butt thus fhe pafs'd to a better World, when only worthy of her, when as if prefageing what was att hand, fhe that very day feavenight (as I noted) furnifh'd herfelfe with the heavenly Viaticum, after an extordinary prepara-tion, preventing the poffible diffadvan-tages of what might furprize her fpi-ritts and diforder her recollection with a moft pious and heavenly addrefs. Nor was this taken notice of onely by thofe who were wittneffes of it fome dayes before

before fhe was brought to bedd, but fignally appeared in that paper which fhe had left in the hands of her in-dear'd Sifter in law Miftrefs Bofcawen, to deliver her Hufband, in cafe of mor-tall accident, which foe foone as it was poffible to compofe his and the vni-verfall grief to any temper, was per-form'd.

" My deare, not knowing how God Allmighty may deale with me, I think it my beft courfe to fettle my affaires, foe as that, in cafe I be to leave this world, noe earthly thing may take vp my thoughts. In the firft place, my dear, beleive me, that of all earthly things you were and are the moft dear to me; and I am convinced that no-body ever had a better or halfe foe good a hufband. I begg your pardon for all my Imperfections, which I am fencible were many; but fuch as I could help, I did endeavour to fubdue, that they
might

might not trouble you : for thofe defects which I could not rectifye in myfelfe, as want of judgement in the management of my family and houfehold affaires, which I owne myfelfe to be very defective in, I hope your good nature will excufe, and not remember to my difadvantage when I am gone. I afk your pardon for the vanitye of my humour, and for being often [more] melancholy and fplenetick than I had caufe to be. I was allwayes afham'd of myfelfe when I was foe, and forry for it, and I hope it will come into the number of thofe faults which I could not help. Now (my dear) God be with thee ; pray God blefs you, and keepe you his faithfull Servant for ever. In him be all thy joy and delight, fatisfaction and comfort, and doe not grieve too much for me, fince I hope I fhall be happy, being very much refign'd to God's will, and leaveing this World with, I hope, in Chrift Jefus, a good Confcience. Now, my

dear,

dear, if you pleafe, permitt me to afk leave to beftow a legacy or two amongft my friends and fervants. In the firft place, if it might be, I could wifh, when the Child I goe with grows of a fitt bignefs, itt might be either with my fifter Bofcawen, or my fifter Penn, for I know they will be carefull of its better Part, which is the cheife thing I am concern'd about. In the next place, I defire you would give B——— [her woman] one hundred pounds (the vfe of which being fix pounds a year, fhe may live att her Ffather's houfe vpon, if fhe will, for I fear fhe will fcarce gett any body to bear with her want of good fervice, as I have done). For my Maid, if fhe doe not marry, I hope fhe will be kept to looke after my Child, when it comes from Nurfe. In the meane tyme, you will give her board wages. For my two footemen, I hope you will gett them places as foone as you can, etc. However, if you be not difpofed

difpofed to keepe them, you will give
them att parting ten pounds a piece.
I defire you will give my Sifters my
fhare of the Queen's Leafe, fifty pounds
a year; itt is betweene them two, my
vnmarryed ones I meane; and to my
Cozen Sarah an hundred pounds in
mony. To my Lady Silvius my great
diamond ring, &c.

" Now, my dear, I have done, if
you pleafe to lay out about an hundred
pounds more in rings for your five
Sifters, to remember me by. I know
nothing more I have to defire of you,
but that you will fometymes think of
me with kindnefs, butt never with too
much griefe. For my Funerall, I defire there may be noe coft beftowed
vpon it att all; butt if I might, I would
begg that my body might lye where I
have had fuch a mind to goe myfelfe,
att Godolphyn, among your freinds. I
beleive, if I were carried by Sea, the
expence

expence would not be very great ; but I don't infift vpon that place, if you think it not reafonable ; lay me where you pleafe.

" Pray, my deare, be kind to that poore Child I leave behind, for my fake, who lov'd you foe well ; butt I need not bidd you, I know you will be foe. If you fhould think fitt to marry againe, I humbly begg that little for- tune I brought, may be firft fettled vpon my Child, and that as long as any of your Sifters live, you will lett it (if they permitt) live with them, for it may be, tho' you will love itt, my fuc- ceffor will not be foe fond of it, as they I am fure will be.

" Now, my deare Child, farewell ; the peace of God, which paffeth all vnderftanding, keepe your heart and mind in the knowledge and love of God and of his Son Jefus Chrift our Lord ;

Lord; and the blessing of God All-mighty, the Father, the Sonn, and the Holy Goft, be with thee, and remaine with thee, ever and ever. Amen."

Then follows what she had intrusted me withall.

This indearing Instance of a truely loyall and admirable Wife were capable of the most noble reflections, foe religious, foe tender, foe discreete, and every way becomeing. That she accuses herselfe of, being fometymes more folemne then vfually young Ladyes are, and which she calls the Spleen, I can by noe meanes admitt a fault: and if her other imperfections, of which she beggs pardon, were but fuch as her want of oeconomique prudence in the management of her family, I dare pronounce her the moft confummate of all the perfections that can adorne or recomend her fex.

I fay

I fay nothing of that wonderfull affection to her Hufband, that made her
foe defireous to mingle her dirt with his
in a dormitorye 300 miles from the reft
of all her Relations, and where to my
knowledge fhe would more contentedly
have paff'd all her dayes with him then
amidft the fplendor of the greateft
Court, and where he might be the
Horizon, all that fhe could or cared to
fee.

The education of her dear Child is
next: Obferve with what care for the
better Part, with what excellent choice
for the perfon to whome fhe recomended
it. Nor does fhe extend her kindnefs
only to her Relations, butt the meaneft
of her Servants. As for the Poore, fhe
had not onely fent thofe good workes
before her, which fhe now enjoyes the
treafure and reward of in Heaven, butt
tooke order they might be continued
after

after her, and ſhe being dead yett ſpeakes.

I might haply have taken it vnkind-ly, if ſhe had named ſoe much as a bro-ther, and left me out; butt the Legatyes ſhe bequeathed, or rather deſired her Huſband to gratifye her in, were only to her Siſters and your Ladyſhipp, ex-cept what ſhe beſtows among her Do-meſtick; to one of which ſhe gave noe leſs then an hundred pounds, and to her owne Siſters the vallue of a thou-ſand; laſtly, to me the honour (att the foote of this Paper) of being mentioned the depoſitarye of her Truſt as I was the diſtributer of her Bounty. Butt which was more obligeing, the ſolemne profeſſion to her Huſband, a little be-fore her Sickneſs, that ſhe knew of no-thing more ſhe had to finiſh or wiſh for in this World, butt that ſhe might doe me ſome ſignall kindneſs. I confeſs ſhe had often both ſaid and written ſoe

to

to me, butt that fhe fhould think of it
as a Concerne doubly indeares her memory. This (fayes that excellent Creature) fhe has left me to doe, and Madam, he has done it, in allowing me
the honour of his freindfhipp, and accepting my little fervices ; for the reft,
I have her Picture in the houfe, and the
Idea of her virtues in my heart, befides
a thoufand expreffions of a religious
and noble Friendfhipp, vnder her owne
fair hand, which I preferve and value
above all fhe could elfe bequeath me.

There was another fmall Pacquett
feal'd vp, which fhe defired by the fu-
perfcription might be burnt, and not
open'd, as accordingly it was perform'd,
and, as I conceive, contained the Cy-
pher onely by which fhe vfually corre-
fponded with her ghoftly Father, the
Deane of Hereford ; or fome particulars, which fhe would not truft her
memory with, in cafe fhe had lived, for

as

as I accquainted your Ladyſhipp, ſhe kept a Catalogue of mercyes, deliverances, ſucceſſes, reſolutions, and other aſſiſtances, for the diſcuſſion of her Conſcience with the moſt accurate niceneſs. Butt I enter not into this Secrett.

Thus began, lived, and ended this incomparable Chriſtian, Virgin, Wife, and Freind, for an emulous example of perfection in all thoſe capacityes. Butt after all I have ſaid, impoſſible will it be to conceive what ſhe was, without endeavouring to imitate and attaine thoſe excellencyes and early virtues which made her what ſhe was : to ſhew you that—, ſomething I have here attempted according to my poore ability; butt he were a rare Artiſt indeed [who] could reach the orriginall, and give thoſe laſt and liveing touches which ſhould make it breathe. But, Madam, that is not to be expreſſed by lights and ſhadows

dows which is alltogeather illuftrious, and has nothing in it darke.

Here, then, Madam, after I have recounted to you her Life,—butt which reaches the profill onely, and wants a world of finifhing,—I fhould, according to the ufuall method, conclude it with her Character, if that accomplifhed peice were not referved for a greater Mafter, and one that could defcribe her mind. All I can pretend to, will hardly reach the out ftrokes, and when I fhall have done my beft, be butt an imperfect copy.

Add this paper (Electra) to the fardle of my other Impertinencyes; butt take heed to the ftepps and progrefs you make; for if I live, I will write your life, att leaft from the firft approaches of our friendfhipp, till I carry it into other Manfions. But becaufe your great humility fhall not fuffer by the admirable

admirable things I muſt ſay of you, nor
the brightneſs of the Subjeƈt be eclipſed
by the defeƈts of the Inſtrument, it ſhall
be under ſuppoſed names, but in veri-
table inſtances; for either wee want ſuch
examples for good writers to exerciſe
their ſtyle and talents on, or good
writers to tranſmitt them to poſteritye.

I know not really how ſhe could doe
the age wee live in more Juſtice, nor
leave that to come a nobler monument
of Gratitude for the Improvements your
Converſation has taught it : whilſt Electra knows this, ſhe will need noe Socrates
or Zeno to ſtand before her ; ſhe re-
veres herſelfe, and can doe nothing below her dignitye. I proteſt to you, the
thought that ſhe is alwayes preſent,
and the contemplation of her vertues, is
more to me than a thouſand dead phi-
loſophers. But wee have a better mo-
nitor, and it were an imbecility infinitely beneath us, to need the veneration
of

of men, when God,—all Eare and Eye, omnifcient and omniprefent,—obferves both our words and actions. Lett us therefore, both, foe fpeak with God as if men heard us, and fo converfe with men as if God faw us.

Behold, Madam, what I once fub-fcribed at the foote of a Letter to this bleffed Creature; and often fhe would fmile at what I ufed to repeate upon this fubject, and as often did I difbeleive my felfe. Far, very far was it from my imagination, farther, infinitely farther from my defires, to furvive (for) this office; who had it conftantly in my wifhes, that fhe might clofe my eyes; butt foe it has pleafed God, that I fhould verifye my prophecy, and on your Ladyfhipp's comand, abfolve my promife together. I have written her Life, and fhould now prefent your Ladyfhip with her Picture: here are Colours, but where is (as I faid) the Mafter?

Mrs. Godolphin.

165

Mafter? She fat indeed fome confiderable tyme to me, and her converfation had been enough to infpire an Artift; but I affure you, there are fome peculiar Graces, which the moft fkillfull doe not arrive to in their moft elaborate and finifhed pieces. And fhe was full of thofe, and fuch as I never yet did fee in any of her fex but in her alone; and am certaine never fhall, unlefs it be in thofe few pieces fhe drew her felfe, whereof your Ladyfhipp is a breathing and illuftrious one, whilft you tread the pathes of her piety and virtues: this, Madam, I pretend to know, and to fhew you from whome I take my meafures.

THE PICTURE.

Lett me firft then recall to your Ladyfhipps remembrance how fhe ufually paffed the day, for an inftance allmoft inimitable in the ftation where
fhe

she was, the Court. I will begin with Sunday the firſt of the weeke.

Were it never ſoe dark, wett, or uncomfortable weather, dureing the ſeverity of winter, ſhe would rarely omit being att the Chappell att 7 a'clock prayers, and if a Comunion day, how late ſoever her attendance were on the Queen, and her owne exterordinary preparation kept her up, ſhe would be dreſſed and att her private Devotions ſome houres before the publick office began. This brings to remembrance what I could not then but ſmile att, that finding one day a long pack thread paſſing through the key hole of her chamber doore, and reaching to her bed's head, (oppoſite to that of your ſiſters, if I be not miſtaken,) and inquireing what it ſingnifyed, I att laſt underſtood, itt had been to awaken her early in the morning, the Centinell, whoſe ſtation was of courſe near the entrance,

trance, being defired to pull it very hard
att fuch an hour, whilft the other extream
was tyed faft about her wrift, fearing
her maid might over fleep her felfe, or
call her later then fhe had appointed.

But befides the monthly Comunions,
fhe rarely miffed a Sunday throughout
the whole Year, wherein fhe did not receive the holy Sacrament, if fhe were
in towne and tollerable health; and I
well know fhe had thofe who gave her
conftant advertifement where it was celebrated upon fome more folemn fefti-
vals, befides not feldome on the weeke
days affifting at one poore creature's or
other; and when fometymes, being in
the Country, or on a Journey, fhe had
not thefe oppertunityes, fhe made ufe
of a devout meditation upon that facred
Miftery, by way of mentall Communion,
foe as fhe was in a continuall ftate of
preparation: and O, with what unfpeak-
able care and nicenefs did fhe ufe to
drefs and trim her foul againft this
                              Heavenly

Heavenly Banquett; with what flagrant devotion at the Altar. I doe affure your Ladyfhipp, I have feen her receive the holy fymbolls, with fuch an humble and melting joy in her countenance, as feem'd to be fomething of tranfport, not to fay angelic—fomething I cannot defcribe: and fhe has her felfe confeffed to me to have felt in her foule fuch influxes of heavenly Joy as have allmoft carryed her into another world; I doe not call them Rapts and Illapfes, becaufe fhe would not have endured to be efteemed above other humble Chriftians; butt that fhe was fometymes vifitted with exterordinary favours I have many reafons to believe: fee what upon another occafion fhe writes to me.

" O, my friend, how happy was I on Sunday laft. By reafon of this foolifh play," (of which I have allready given your Ladyfhipp an account,) " moft imperfect were my preparations, and yett

yett I do not remember that God was ever more gracious to me but once afore; and indeed that tyme I had foe great a fence of my owne unworthynefs and the wonderfull condefcencion and love of God, that I had like to have fallen flat on my face; butt that excepted this was the moft refrefhing. O Jefu, (faid I,) how happy are wee, how bleffed, that have the Lord for our God. And you, bleffed Angells, who are prefent att thefe affemblyes, admireing the heavenly bounty, I tell you I was even diffolved with love to God. And yett, after all this, what wretched things wee are: I was drowfy att Church, wandering in my thoughts, and forgettfull of thefe favours that very day; and great caufe I had to lament my finns of even that day. Thus I acknowledge to you Gods love to my poore foule, and my foule ingratitude to him; that you may pray for the continuance of the one, and I truft the other will

will in tyme grow lefs." See this humble foule. But I fubjoyne one more.

" I blefs God," (fays fhe,) " I grow dayly lefs fond of the world, more thankfull to God, lefs folicitous for outward things, and more thirfty after the bleffed Sacrament, not as I was wont, nor becaufe I hold it my duty, but out of an ardent defire to commemorate my Saviour's death, and to be againe entertained with the wonderfull pleafure that I feele there, and noe .where elfe. All worldly joyes, all fplendid ornaments, titles and honour, would I bring to the feete of my crucifyed Saviour."

Nor did this bleffed Saint hear the word of God with lefs reverence : imploying that day allmoft intirely in pious meditations, and never failing to recollect what fhe had heard, with that diligence, that there was not a Sermon
but

but what fhe had abftracted, writeing downe the principall heads of the whole difcourfe, foe foone as fhe came from Church (if fhe had leifure), or, to be fure, in the evening ere fhe flept; and this courfe fhe never omitted, nor to repeat what fhe obferved of moft inftructive: and her memory was foe happy, as nothing materiall efcaped her. This, to my aftonifhment, I can teftifye.

How would this Lady rejoyce att the approach of the Lord's day. She has often told me, fhe felt another foule in her, and that there was nothing more afflicted her, than thofe impertinent vifitts on Sunday Evenings, which fhe avoided with all imaginable induftry; whilft yett feldome did fhe pafs one without goeing to vifitt, pray by, or inftruct fome poore religious Creature or other, tho' it were to the remoteft part of the Towne, and fometymes, if the

the feafon were inviteing, walke into
the fields or Gardens to contemplate
the workes of God. In a word, fhe
was allwayes foe folemnly chearfull upon that day, and foe devout, that without lookeing into the Kalender, one
might have read it in her countenance.
Thus was the Sunday taken up in
prayers, hearing, receiveing, meditateing on the word and workes of God,
acts of Charity, and other holy exercifes,
without the leaft formalitye or con-
fufion, becaufe fhe had caft all her affairs into fuch a method, as rendered it
delightfull as well as holy.

Vpon feftivall dayes, fhe never
omitted the offices of the Church; takeing thofe opportunityes of vifitting
poore fick people, relieveing and com-
forting them; and then would lengthen
her evening retirements with proper
meditations on the Myftery, or come-
moration; for which fhe had of her owne
collection,

collection, appofite entertainments: butt then upon indicted faft dayes, befides what fhe weekly fett apart her felfe, and (efpecially before the Monthly Co- munions) how exterordinary were her receffes and devotions on every Friday, when fhe rarely ftirr'd out of her little Oratorye butt to publique prayers, and then would end the evenings in vifitts of charity; and did for feverall years obferve the Lent with ftrictnefs, both as to her reflections and devotion, till finding it much impaire her health and delicate conftitution, fomething of thofe fevere mortifications fhe was per- fwaded to abate; only the holy weeke her excercifes was extended to all the parts of duty, and more folemn prepa- ration, fpent in an uninterrupted courfe of penitentiall and exterordnary devo- tion, yett without fuperftitious ufages, or the leaft moroffnefs.

Vpon fuch Anniverfaryes, fhe would be

be early att the Chappell ; and fometymes I have knowne her fhutt up in
the Church after the publick offices
have been ended, without returneing
to her Chamber att all, to prevent impertinent vifitts and avocations, and
that fhe might fpend the day in continuall devotion. With thefe aufterityes
paffed fhe the dayes of abftinence ; nay,
though it fell upon a feftivall, and
when others thought themfelves att liberty. This recalls to me an anfwer
which fhe once return'd me, kindly re-
proveing her for a feverity on a certaine holy day.

" As to fafting on a feftivall," (fayes
fhe,) " I had not done it, butt that I
had for it the opinion of a learned and
reverend Bifhopp, who told me it was
not a fafting day of our owne makeing ; wee might, when a faft and a
feaft of the Church meete, feaft att
Church and faft att home ; which I did,
and

and it was a good day with me. I could be content never to dyne foe long as I live, foe as I might fpend every day like that."

By this your Ladyfhipp may fee how well advifed fhe was in all fhe did, and what exterordnary guft and fatisfaction fhe received in her devout intercourfes.

Butt the truth is, not onely did fhe faft on dayes of Indiction, and fuch as the Church enjoynes : every meale was a day of abftinence with her, for as fhe feldome eate of above one or two difhes, where there were great plenty, foe very rarely would fhe have any fauces, and comonly chofe the dryeft and leaneft morfells ; and frequently have I knowne her deny her appetite things which I am certaine fhe lov'd, foe as I have made it now and then a little quarrell, for treating her felfe no better, confider-ing her tender fabrick, early rifeing,
tedious

tedious and late watchings, laborious
devotions, and not feldome even to
fainting in her retirements. Butt fhe
would tell me fmileingly, that fhe was
as ftrong as a lion ; and though I ma-
nifeftly perceived the contrary, both by
her countenance and other circumftances, that thefe aufterityes did her
injury, fhe would difguife it with an
induftry foe naturall, and putt fuch life
and chearfullnefs into her lookes and
mine, as has made me call to mind what
wee read of Daniell and his companions,
(Dan. 1,) who after their afcetick
foode, looked fairer and in better point
then all the reft who eat of the Royall
portion. " I can be fatt," (fhe would
tell me,) " in three dayes when I will."

I forgott to remember your Ladyfhipp, of her imploying moft part of
Lent in workeing for poore people,
cutting out and makeing waiftcoates
and other neceffary coverings, which
fhe

she conftantly diftributed amongft them, like another Dorcas, fpending much of her tyme, and no little of her money, in relieving, vifitting, and enquireing of them out.   And whilft fhe was thus bufy with her needle, fhe would commonly have one or other read by her, through which means, and a happy memory, fhe had allmoft the whole Scriptures by heart, and was foe verfed in Doctor Hammond's Annotations and other practicall bookes, Controverfyes, and Cafes, as might have ftocked fome who pafs for noe fmall Divines; not to mention fundry divine penitentiall and other Hymns, breathing of a Spiritt of holynefs, and fuch as fhew'd the tendernefs of her heart, and wonderfull love to God.

Thus fpent fhe the Sunday, feafts, or fafts ; nor were the exterordnary weeke dayes other than Sundayes with her when none came to interrupt her courfe,

courfe, which in fome particulars was
conftant and unintermitted. For the
Sun had not yett drawne the Curtaines
of his purple bed, whofe rifeing fhe oft
prevented, and even fometymes the
Morning watch, when this holy Virgin,
wakeing, after a fhort Ejaculation to
the Father of lights for the refrefhment
fhe had received, thus excites herfelfe,—

"*Up and be doeing, fleepe no more;*
 Hark! who is knocking att the doore?
 Arife, my faire one, come away;
 For thee I waite: arife, and pray.
 Shake off thy Sleepe; behold, 'tis I!
 Canft thou love that, when I am by?
 Vaine thoughts, prefume not to come
   near,
 You'l find no entertainements here;
 My Love has fworne—her vows are
   paft—
 That I fhall be her firft and laft.
 Rife then, my deareft, come and fee
 What pleafureas are referv'd for thee.
       I come

I come, dear Lord.   Behold I rife.
Thee, I beyond all pleafures prize."

Doe not imagine I am purfueing a
romance, or in a rapture myfelfe, whilft
I call her up with this angelick Hymne,
fince I can affure your Ladyfhipp 'tis
butt what I find under her owne hand,
and amongft thofe devout tranfports
and compofures of hers, which I am
certaine were her owne: and when
fhe was in health, fhe would be call'd
whilft it was yett darke, to feeke her
Lord, like thofe holy women that went
early to the Sepulcher.

Noe fooner was fhe defcended from
her bed, butt fhe fell on her knees in
profound adoration; and all the tyme of
her dreffing,—which for the moft part
fhe finifh'd of her felfe without other
help,—her mayd was reading fome part
of Scripture to her, and when her affiftance was neceffary, fhe would take the
booke

booke herſelfe, and read to her maid;
thus continually imploy'd ſhe her meditations, till ſhe was fully dreſſ'd;
which ſhe would be in a very little
tyme, even to all the agreeable circumſtances becomeing her, becauſe indeed
ſhe became every thing, and this early
riſeing and little indulgence to her eaſe,
made her looke like a flower, lovely,
and freſh, and full of health : being in
this poſture, ſhe withdrew to private
devotion in her cloſett, till her ſervant
advertiſed her it was tyme to goe to
the Chappell, where ſhe was ever with
the firſt of the devout ſex, were it never
ſoe wett, cold, and darke, even before
day breake, in midſt of winter.

Return'd from Chappell, ſhe would
ſhutt her ſelfe upp in her little Oratorye
againe, where, till the Queene requir'd
her attendance, (for I now deſcribe her
as ſhe was att Court,) ſhe was either
imployed in reading ſome holy booke,
or

or getting some Chapter or Psalmes by heart, such as she had collected abundance of the most edifyeing; neither omitted she to pray constantly with her small family, which she tooke great care to instruct upon all occasions. Nor did her forenoone devotion determine here: she not seldome might be found in the Chappell att ten a'Clock in the longer office. Nay, and I have sometymes mett her above in his Majestyes little oratorye before dinner, if conveniently she could slipp away from the mixt Company of the withdrawing Roome, whilst the Queene satt out; and this she did, not out of singularity or superstitious devotion, or that she thought herselfe obliged to it, butt (as she has told me) to avoid occasions of idle and impertinent discourse, which was allmost unavoidable in the Ante-Chambers.

Soe soone as her Majestye had dyned, (if

(if it were her duty and turne to wayte,) and that fhe had alfoe taken her repaft, if fhe owed no formall vifitts, or were not interrupted by others, fhe ufually fpent the afternoone in workeing with her needle, which was comonly (butt efpetially, as I noted, in Lent tyme,) makeing Coates and Garments for poore people, and fometymes for great and rich, for there was nothing but [what] her delicate fingers could doe, and fhe had an Invention and fancy foe elegant and pretty, that when there was any thing exterordinary to be done in fuiteing Ornaments and adjufting Ladyes' matters att Court, tho' fhe affected none of this her felfe, happy was the moft illuftrious of the Circle, [who] could have her to drefs and fett them out.

She was fometymes engaged to pafs the after dynner att Cards, efpecially when fhe came to Berkley Houfe, (where was great refort,) more to comply

ply with others, than that fhe tooke the leaft delight in it; and tho' being comonly extreamly fortunate, and very fkillfull, fhe comonly rofe a winner, and allwayes referved her winnings for the poore, itt was yett amongft the greateft afflictions of her life, when, to comply with fome perfons of Qualitye, fhe fatt any thing long att itt. How many fad complaints has fhe made to me of this particular: I tell you fhe looked on it as a Calamity and fubjection infupportable. Butt neither did this nor any other confideration detaine her from being prefent att publick prayers att 3 or 4 a'clock, for fhe would then break off, and happ'ly take that opportunitye of makeing fome vifitt, if fhe had any to pay.

She had her houres alfoe for reading hiftorye and diverfions of that nature; butt allwayes fuch as were choice, profittable, and inftructive, and fhe had devoured

voured an incredible deale of that folid knowledge, and could accompt of it to admiration; foe as I have even beene aftonifhed to find fuch an heape of ex-cellent things and materiall obfervations collected and written with her owne hand, many of which (fince her being with God) came to myne, for befides a world of admirable prayers and pieces of flagrant devotion, meditations, and difcourfes on various fubjects, (which fhe compof'd) there was hardly a booke fhe read that fhe had not common placed, as it were, or taken fome re-markable note of; add this to the Diary of her owne life, actions, refolutions, and other circumftances, of which I fhall give fome fpecimen. She had contracted the intire hiftorye of the Scriptures, and the moft illuftrious examples, fentences, and precepts, digefted under appofite and proper heads; and collected to-geather the refult of every Article of the Apoftles' Creed, out of Bifhopp Pear-
fon's

son's excellent Treatise. I have allready spoken of her Sermon Notes;
butt to give a juft Account of her Letters, they are foe many and in fo excellent
naturall and eafy a ftyle, that as for their
number, one would beleive fhe did nothing elfe butt write, foe for their weight
and ingenuity, that fhe ought to doe
nothing elfe; and foe eafyly did her
Invention flow, that I have feene her
write a very long letter without once
takeing off her penn (butt to dipp it),
and that with exterordnary Judgment;
they were cogent, pathetick, and obligeing, and allwayes about doeing fome
kind office, or Religious Correfpond-
ence. Nor lefs was fhe indefatigable
in reading; feldome ftirring abroad
without fome good booke about her,
that if by any accident fhe were to attend or be alone, fhe might lofe no
tyme; and indeed the tone of her voice
(when fhe read to others) was foe fuited
to all the paffions and figures either of

reading

reading or difcourfe, that there was nothing more charmeing then to heare her
recite with fuch a Spiritt and Judgment as the periods fell.   'Tis hardly
to be imagined, the talent fhe peculiarly
had in repeating a comicall part or acting it, when in a chearfull humour and
amongft fome particular friends, fhe
would fometymes divert them; and I
have heard her pronounce a Sermon
in French which fhe had heard preached
by a fryar in Paris vpon the profeffion
of a Nun, att which fhe was prefent,
that really furprized me.   Thofe who
have obferv'd the fantaftick motion of
thofe Zealotts in the pulpitt would have
feen in this Lady's action, invention, and
preachment, the prettieft and moft innocent Mimick in the World, and have
really beleived it had been the Enthufiaft
himfelfe, butt for his frock and face, that
had infpired her : certainely fhe was
the moft harmelefs and diverting Creature in nature.   Butt as her witt was
infinite

infinite, and in Converfation far fuperior
to any of her fex, foe to curb it, had
fhe fuch perpetuall apprehenfions of
God's omniprefence, that fhe induftrioufly fuppreffed it. I could tell your
Ladyfhipp of fome artificiall helps fhe
ufed, to keep her allwayes in mind of
it: thus fhe would pin up fome papers, as it were negligently, in places
where fhe moft frequently ufed to be,
with fome Character in it, or halfe word,
that fignifyed to her fome particular
duty or Caution; and though I never
came to know this from her felfe, yett
by fome obfervations which I made, I
am confident of what I fay. Butt this
fhe did to curb and reftraine as (I faid)
her fprightfull witt in perfect humility,
and out of feare and tendernefs left
fhe might offend; tho' never was Creature more difcreetely referv'd, or that
better vnderftood when and what it
was fitt to fpeake and entertaine her
friends.

To

To preferve her felfe then in this humble temper, and affift her more minute Confeffions, fhe kept (as I have hinted) an account of her actions and refolutions, as fince her deceafe I find. In this it was fhe fett downe her Infirmityes fhe laboured vnder, what deliverances fhe had from danger, what favour received, what Methods fhe refolved to take for the imployment of her tyme, and obligations laid vpon her felfe to performe what fhe foe refolved, which doubtlefs was a Courfe to keep her clofe to duty, as well as the frequent Counfells of her Ghoftly father upon all difficultyes by the conftant Intercourfe of Letters, foe as fhe [was] feldome in fufpence, what fhe ought to doe upon any difficulty which might concerne her: and this infinitely contributed to the Chearfullnefs of her Spiritts and interior peace; fhe was really foe afraid that others fhould think

too

too well of her, that fhe has fometymes
bitterly accufed herfelfe, and was wont
to fend me an anniverfary account of
her faileings and Infirmityes, in which
God knows there were very few, with
a gratefull remembrance to God of her
Improvements, which I knew to be
much greater then fhe would acknowledge, defireing both advice and prayers
for her.

As in the Morning, foe in the Evening, itt was even fome exterordinary
and indifpenfable buiffnefs which att
any tyme hindered her from the Church
office, which if fhe miffed att three a'
clock, fhe would be fure to find att fix,
whether fhe were abroad or att home;
and after that as conftantly retired fome
competent tyme before Supper for recollection, Reading and private devotion; and would fometymes walk abroad
to contemplate the workes of God, for
which fhe was furnifh with proper meditations,

ditations, which fhe could extend out
of her owne ftock, as I can witnefs, to
my fingular edification and no fmall
admiration : there was really nothing
fhe caft her Eye upon, butt inftead of
impertinent wandring fhe would derive
fome holy ufe from.

"I wifh you here betymes," (one
day writeing to me,) " that wee may
walk together. I fancy I could talk'
of God for ever; and, indeed, what
elfe can wee fpeake of butt our God,
of whome wee never can fay enough :"
for Tuefday being ufually the day I
vifitted her of courfe, whether wee
walked into the Gardens, the fields, or
within doores, the moft agreeable converfation to her, was the contemplation
of the workes of God; [or] the contrive-
ing how to bring about fome charitable
office; and as fhe was ftrangely happy
in compofing differences, foe was fhe
of foe lucky addrefs and univerfally beloved,

loved, that what fhe undertooke fhe
feldome failed of accomplifhing. Generous as fhe was, and foe obligeing to
her freinds, there hardly paffed a day in
which fhe had not done fome fignall
kindnefs : nor difdained fhe the meaneft Circumftances, foe fhe might doe
good ; not to omitt how refolute fhe
was in other dutyes. Nor in all thefe
pious Labours, [was fhe] the leaft troublefome, fcrupulous, fingular, or morofe,
butt [of] the moft eafy and chearfull
converfation in the world.

Thus paffed fhe the Evenings, till
Supper ; which fhe for the moft part refufed her felfe, fpending that tyme in her
oratory ; and if fhe did come downe,
eating fpareingly, retired againe foe
foone as decently fhe could difengage
her felfe to pray with her little family,
and finifh the reft of her private courfe
before fhe went to repofe. This your
Ladyfhipp knows and could fpeake to
much

much better then my felfe, whilft you were fellow virgins and companions in holy dutyes; and thus lived fhe to God and to her felfe.   Let us now take a view how fhe converfed with others, Domefticks and Friends, after fhe was a Wife, and had a family to governe.

It is ufually faid of marryed people, " fuch a one has altered her condition," indeed, foe had fhee.   But in noe fort her Courfe.   Itt could not be faid of this paire, that thofe who are marryed cared for the things of this world how they might pleafe one another, for never was there Lady pleafed foe well as when fhe was careing for the things of the Lord, and this fhe did (if any ever did) without diftraction, knowing that fhe could never pleafe her hufband better then when fhe was pleafing God; foe as fhe was, (I may truely fay,) the fame [as] a wife and a virgin.   And fuch a Marriage it was, I am perfwaded St.
Paul

Paul himſelfe would have preferred
above the celibate he ſoe highly co-
mended, butt for which he had noe
command, but ſpoke on ſuppoſition.

She was none of thoſe who would
have excuſed her comeing to the divine
and royall feaſts becauſe ſhe had marryed an huſband; ſlacking in nothing
of her former zeale and labours of love,
without the leaſt impeachment to her
domeſtick Charge. Soe dextrouſly ſhe
knew to reconcile both thoſe dutyes,
that I beleive there never was family
more an houſehold of faith, never perſons linked togeather in a more honourable, happy, and eaſy bond: for as ſhe
was an excellent Chriſtian, ſhe was a
noe leſs unparalleld wife; I need not
therefore deſcribe this vertue to your
Ladyſhipp, or call that complaiſance
which was the height of a moſt vertuous
affection; and reciprocall; for never were
two perſons ſoe framed for one another's

ther's difpofitions, never lived paire in more peace and harmony; and yett, tho' this converfation was the moft noble and becomeing in the world, without troublefome fondnefs, yet fhe could not conceale the affliction fhe fuffered when he was abfent, as when he had been fometymes fent abroad by his Majeftye, upon diverfe publick concerns of State, nor the Joy that fo fpread it felfe in her countenance, and agreeable humour, when he was prefent. In a word, fhe was converfation as well as Companion for a wife and excellent perfon, foe as if ever two were created for each other, and marriages, as they fay, made in heaven, this happy paire were of the number. O irreparable lofs, never to be repaired on this fide that bleffed place.

For the prudent management of her domeftick affaires, fhe was not to learne what ever might become the graveft

or

or [moſt] experienced Matron as well as
Miſtreſs. She had ſoone made choice of
ſuch ſervants, and putt all things in ſuch
order, as nothing was more eaſy, me-
thodicall, and quiett; without ſingularity or affectation; nothing more de-
cent and honourable. She provided
them bookes to read, prayers to uſe by
themſelves, and conſtantly inſtructed
them herſelfe in the principles of Religion; tooke care for their due receiveing of the holy Sacrament, and was in
a word the beſt miſtreſs in the world:
wittneſs her bountifull remembrance of
them att her death, of which I have
allready ſpoken.

She tooke exact Accompt of her
dayly expenſes, which every Saturday
ſhe uſed to ſumme up, and never went
on ſcore; ſoe juſt and provident ſhe was;
makeing that a delight which others
looke on as a Burthen,—namely, the
care of her family, which ſhe would
goe

goe through with an hardineſs and maſ-
culine virtue, ſoe farr was ſhe from being nice and delicate, and it infinitely
became her. None knew better then
ſhe to buy and to chuſe what was fitt ;
tempering a diſcreet frugalitye, with a
generous hand and a large heart ; and
if in any thing profuſe itt was in her
Charitye.

And thus I have ſhewed your Ladyſhipp how ſhe lived to God and to
herſelfe ; I have now to add how ſhe
converſed with her Neighbours, whom
ſhe loved as herſelfe.

Your Ladyſhipp is of too generous a
Soule to forgett that particular affection
ſhe bore you to the laſt, the eſteeme
ſhe had of your excellent ſiſter and Relations : and methinks I ſtill ſee the concerne ſhe ſhewed, when you were prepareing to goe into Holland about this
tyme, becauſe her ſolicitude for your
profperity

profperity was accompanyed with a tender friendſhipp; which I find you would keepe in memory by the Inſtances you make to one, whome you juſtly think have noe leſs gratefull diſpoſition to celebrate her vertues.

Indeed never was any Creature more obligeing to her friends and Relations; to whoſe Civilityes, that ſhe might be juſt, ſhe not only kept a Catalogue of thoſe ſhe had a more particular eſteeme of, butt would ſtudy all imaginable wayes to be ſerviceable to them. Wee both are wittneſſes of the paines ſhe would undergoe to proſelyte vaine or indifferent Chriſtians, and with what an admirable addreſs ſhe did it; without the leaſt diminution of her ſelfe, or mean complyance to gaine friendſhipp with eſteeme; tho' ſhe was ſcrupulouſly carefull not to multiply accquaintances, conſidering the precious moments that are loſt in impertinent and formal viſitts,

fitts, and therefore reduceing [them] to
a felect and choice number. Nothing in
the world did more afflict her than the
trifling Converfation of fome whome of
Decency fhe was obliged to bear with,
whilft there was not a vifitt which fhe
returned to fuch, butt with a fecrett defigne, how fhe might either reclaime
thofe who were lefs referved and circum-
fpect, or confirme and incourage thofe
that were more. Never fhould you
hear her fpeake to the difadvantage of
an abfent perfon; butt if others did,
fhe would be either filent and fay nothing, unlefs where fhe could excufe
them, or endeavour to divert the difcourfe. In every thing elfe fhe had
a wonderfull complacency of nature;
which was infinitely improved by Religion, and a kind of univerfall Charitye,
foe as to accomodate her felfe to all innocent humours. She would fing, and
play, and act, and recite, and difcourfe
prettyly and innocently a thoufand
harmelefs

harmelefs and ingenious purpofes to re-
creat old and melancholy perfons, and
divert the younger. She had kindnefs
and good nature to fitt by the fick and
peevifh, read and pray by them with
infuperable patience and chearfullnefs,
and comply even with little Children;
fhe played att any the moft difficult
games fuiteable to their Converfation,
and that fkillfully : nor was there any
refifting her agreeable way and govern-
ing fpiritt; foe that (as I noted) the
greateft Ducheffes and Ladyes of the
Court fought her friendfhipp and affiftance vpon any occafion of folemn pomp,
Mafque, Ball, or exterordinary appearance, becaufe of a certaine peculiar
fancy and addrefs fhe had in fuiteing,
dreffing, and continueing things of Or-
nament, with universall approbation,
whilft in all thefe Complyances, fhe
was watchfull of opportunityes to in-
ftill fomething of vertue and Religion,
as well by her difcourfe as example,
and

and in fuch a manner, as not only avoided the Cenfure of Impertinence and fingularity, butt which more endeared her to them. What fhall I fay? fhe had all the pretty arts and innocent ftratagems imaginable, of mingling ferious things on all occafions, feafoning even her diverfions with fomething of Religion; which, as fhe would manage it, putt to rebuke all their ftocks of rayllery, foe as nothing was more agreeable than her Company where ever fhe came. Indeed there was nothing proofe againft the abundance of her witt and piety : fhe made vertue and holynefs a chearfull thing, lovely as her felfe; and even in the Court, how many of the greateft there, were made to looke upon Religion as a ferious thing, yett confiftent with their poft. Butt this I need not recount to your Ladyfhipp, there are yett fome (and more I wifh there were) who owe their tincture to this Lady, and will, I

hope,

hope, retaine it; foe as, if ever it were
an holy Court, 'twas when this Saint
was the life of it. 'Twere eafy to fhew
whome, by her Councell and addrefs,
fhe had refcued; fome from fatall preci-
pices in that giddy Station; others,
whome fhe has inftructed, that were
Ignorant or carelefs; fome, that fhe
gained to a fevere Courfe, who were
liftning to folly and ruine: in a word,
it was the pleafure of her life and the
buiffnefs of the day, to caft about how
fhe might improve it to thofe advantages. O, were the Courts of Princes
adorn'd and furnifh'd with fuch a Circle
wee fhould call it Heaven on Earth,
and converfe with Angells. Butt, to
juftifye this and all that I have affirmed
concerning the piety of her thoughts,
the paffion fhe had to improve others,
the richnefs of her Invention, naturall
Eloquence, and beauty of her Style, I
have no more to doe then to mind your
Ladyfhipp of a Letter, written by this
Saint,

Saint, when ſhe was now gone from
Court, of which I am well aſſured you
are beſt accquainted, and can yett perhapps produce the orriginall; for my
part I never read it butt I looke upon
it as inſpired with an apoſtolick ſpiritt.

" Deare Children, ſince you are both
ſoe lowly in your owne Eyes, as to
make uſe of me in a thing which either
of you would have done better, butt
that you diſtruſt your ſelfes,—namely,
the paraphraſes vpon the prayer lately
ſent you, I thought my ſelfe obliged
deepely to conſider it againe, and haveing done ſoe, cannott ſatisfy my leſs,
unleſs I ſett downe with Pen and Ink
what my opinion is of it. As to your
dreſſing, I can't beleive the Doctor
meant there ſhould be any neglect of
that beauty God has given you, ſoe it
be done with this Caution, firſt, that
you deſigne to captivate none for any
ſatisfaction you take in the number of
Lovers

Lovers or in the Noife of a larger
traine of Admirers than other young
women have, butt purely for an honeft
defigne of difingageing your felves as
foone as you can from the place you
are in, in an honorable way ; and when
ever you fee any young Man, whome
in your hearts you cannot beleive will
prove that perfon I fpeak of, or any
marryed Man, whome you know cannot, with fuch a one St. Paul fayes,
you ought not to converfe in the leaft ;
I meane, if [it is] poffible to be avoided,
and in this age, you know, women are
not foe wonderfully folicited that have
the vertue and modefty of you two.
That good fervice the Ladys of other
principles have done you, that men
fooner find their Error, and without
much difficulty fufpected converfations
may be avoided.

" Indeed, it would be a moft dread-
full fight att the laft day, to fee any
man

man condemned upon your accounts;
and yett fuch a thing may be, and yett
you honeſt; for if you willingly conſent
men ſhould looke upon you and follow
you, you are acceſſary to that ſinn in St.
Mathew, 'Who ever lookes on a woman to luſt after her, hath committed
Adultery with her allready in his heart.'
Soe that my opinion is, that mankind, if
they make any particular applications,
tho' they don't make love, be, as much
as you can, avoided. As to your Converſation, there is nothing forbidden
butt what is either prophane, or unjuſt,
or indevout; I meane, the encourage-
ing of any of that in others, by ſeeme-
ing well pleaſed with it. 'Tis true, wee
ſhould not preach in the withdrawing
Roome, butt wee muſt, by our lookes,
ſhew that wee fear God, and that wee
dare not hear any thing to his prejudice,
nor any thing filthy, or that tends to
the prejudice of our Neighbour; and
where any of theſe are found, there, as
much

much as ever wee can, to avoid them. As to what wee fay our felves, the fame Rules are to be obferved; and wee muft take care that wee talke not to be the wittieft in the Company; to accquire praife to ourfelves above our Neighbours. Wee may divert people, and be innocently merry; but then wee muft not' defigne praife to our felves, nor pleafe our felves (if wee have it) in the thoughts of it, butt in fome fhort and filent prayer, defire God to keepe us low in our owne Eyes, as ' Lord, make me poore in fpiritt, that I may inheritt the kingdome of Heaven,' or by calling to mind that faying of St. Paul; ' What haft thou which thou didft not receive, and if thou haft received it, why doft thou boaft?' In fhort, wee muft talke, to divert others, not to gaine applaufe to our felves; and if there be any that are able and willing to doe it, lett us not be impatient to preferr them before us. Butt this is butt fometymes

to

to be done; 'tis not a fault if you
fhould not allwayes be foe willing to
keep filence whilft others fpeake.

" As to your retirement after you
come in, 'tis only to examine the day,
and if you have been faulty, in all humility to acknowledge it to Allmighty
God, and what ever the fault has been,
to read fome portion of Scripture which
concerns it, if you can find any; if not,
to read fome Chapter in St. John's Gofpell, efpecially the 15, or 16, or 17th,
&c. that doe moft divinely fett forth
the Love of God to us. The reafon
why I urge this, is, that your forrow for
fin may proceed from the fence you
have of God's great mercy and love to
us; and that Confideration will melt
your hearts, and keepe you clofe, and
make you defire to draw near him;
but Hell terrifyes, and damnation
amazes, and I am never the better for
thofe reflections.

" And

" And after this is paſſ'd, you both being Good, and friends as well as Siſters,
will doe well to contrive togeather how
you may defeate the Divell, and make
Solomon's words true, that 'two are better then one.' After this, in God's name,
I know no harme,—if your devotions of
the day and taſk that you aſſigne your
ſelves are over,—butt that you may be
as chearfull as your Innocence can make
you, which in both is very great.

" As to one particular in the dreſs, I
think I have not ſpoken concerneing
the expenſive part. Butt that only concerns ——, and Mrs. ——, whoſe
purſes are ſmall, that they take care,
upon noe account whatſoever, they ex-
ceed what their penſion is; for noe
duty to the Queene, in makeing a ſhew
behind her, can excuſe one from Juſtice
to our Neighbour, before that God in
whoſe preſence wee walke, and [who]
                                    will

will avenge the Caufe of the wronged. Butt I am fenfible not only this laft, butt all I have faid, has been not onely (as to my part) filly, butt as to yours, fuperfluous, only Love and Goodwill I dare fay will plead my excufe before two foe good young Creatures for a greater fault than this, and therefore not doubting but I am forgiven, I will [end] with a prayer drawne from the Sermon wee heard this morning.

" That you two, who have foe glorioufly and foe refolutely fett your felves to ferve God in your younger dayes, may continue to be ftill what you are, examples of vertue and modefty in a Court, dutifull to your Mifftrefs, obedient and loveing to your Mother, affectionate to each other, and charitable to all the world. Befides, may you be wife virgins, haveing Oyle in your Lamps ready prepar'd to meete the Bridegroome. May you be burning and

and fhineing lights in the midft of a crooked and perverfe Generation, and as the Minifter faid this day, 'May you, as Samuel, and David, Jofiah, Timothy, and St. John, be wholly dedicated to Gods Service, as was the firft; zealous for his Glory, as was the fecond; conftantly feeking the God of your fathers, as was the third; well inftructed in Scriptures, as was the fourth; and at laft may you (as St. John was) be admitted into the Bofome of our Dear Jefus, where you will have your fhort youth turned into Eternity, your earthly treafure to an heavenly, and your worldly greatnefs and power exchang'd for a Crowne of Glory.' Amen with all my heart."

And now, O bleffed Saint, how doft thou fhine above! What a Circle of Starrs diadems thy Temples! what a Jubilation amongft the Angells at thy accefs into the Glorious Hierarchy! Verily,

Verily, Madam, I have had thoughts
above the world, when I fometymes
confidered the life of this excellent
Creature, her rare examples, happy
fuccefs, and the fruites which have been
planted and cultivated by her holy In-
duftrye and labour of Love, were it by
her beauty, by her witt, her Converfation, her prayers and devotions, her
zeal and pious Infinuations, her example or peculiar addreffe; being wily,
fhe caught them by Craft, and as I faid,
I would fometymes call her the fifherefs
of her fex. What fhall I add? She
was fortunate in all fhe fett her hand to,
becaufe fhe laid out all thefe perfections
in the fervice of God, the winning of
foules; and great, great is her reward.

Nor did this confine her only to the
Court, amongft the Great. I have allready told how diligently fhe would inquire
out the poore and miferable, even [in]
Hofpitalls, humble Cells and Cottages,
whither

whither I have fometymes accompanied
her, as farr as the very fkirts and ob-
fcure places of the Towne, among whom
fhe not only [gave] liberall almes, but
phyfitians and phyfick fhe would fend
to fome, yea, and adminifter Remedyes
herfelfe, and the meaneft offices. She
would fit and read, inftruct and pray,
whole afternoones, and tooke care for
their fpirituall releif by procureing a
Minifter of Religion to prepare them
for the holy Sacrament, for which purpofe fhe not only carryed and gave them
bookes of Salvation and Devotion, but
had herfelfe collected diverfe Pfalmes
and Chapters proper to be read and
ufed vpon fuch occafions. How many
naked poore Creatures fhe covered! I
have by me one Lift of no fewer then
twenty three, whome fhe cladd at one
tyme; and your Ladyfhipp may remember, and I have allready noted, for
whome fhe wrought with her owne
hands.

To

To affift her then in the difpofeing
of thefe and inumerable other Charityes, there was a poore religious Wid-
dow, whome your Ladyfhipp knew fhe
had a more particular Confidence in.
How fhe found her out, I never in-
formed my felfe, but well remember a
paffage of fomething exterordinary that
happened to her concerning a Voice
which fhe folemnly affirmed had fpoken
to her, being once att prayers in the
Church and in great diftrefs. I fhall
fay nothing as to that, but that it was
this pious and humble Creature, whofe
diligence fhe vfed, to informe her of fick
and miferable people, who accompanyed her to their Habitations, and
brought them Cloathes, Mony and Me-
dicines, and whereof they fpent whole
dayes in devotion togeather. By her
it was fhe diftributed weekly penfions,
looked after orphan Children, put them
to fchoole, vifitted the prifons, out of
which

which (amongſt diverſe others,) ſhe had
redeemed a diſſolute ſon of hers, that
coſt a very conſiderable ſumme, as ſhe
had paid the debts, and indeed wholly
maintained the Mother to her dyeing
day, tho' being taken with a dead palſy,
and in a manner bed ridden, a year or
two before.   She ſurvived her Bene-
factreſs, but not her bounty : thus
when ſhe went into Ffrance, ſhe ordered
me to continue many other penſions
which ſhe gave, and I could give you
an account of what houſe rent ſhe paid
for indigent houſkeepers, what Appren-
tices ſhe put forth, and your Ladyſhipp remembers, and I have allready
touched, the little Child ſhe kept allwayes with her, and cheriſhed to the
laſt. Soe ſedulous was ſhe in theſe acts
of Charity, that from the tyme I could
calculate, ſhe had begun and perſiſted
in this Courſe from a Child her ſelfe :
and for the laſt 7 Years of her life, I
can ſpeake of my owne knowledge,
that

that her liberality was foe difpropor-
tion'd to her Revenue, that I have
fometymes called it profufion, at which
fhe would fmile, and bid me take no
care.   What fhe herfelfe diftributed
more privately I know not, but fure I
am it was a great deale more then ever
fhe would difcover, takeing all the Cau-
tions imaginable, that nothing fhe did
of this nature fhould be knowne, no not
to her left hand what her right hand
did, and therefore often would fhe herfelfe walk out alone and on foote, and
fafting, and in midft of winter, (when
it was hardly fitt to fend a fervant out,)
to minifter to fome poore creatures fhe
had found out, and perhaps whome no
body knew of befides, foe far had her
love to God and piety to others overcome nature and the delicate tendernefs
of her fex and conftitution.

See then what I find in her Diarye,
among the Refolutions (as I faid) fhe
was

was wont to fet downe in her owne hand. It feemes fhe had loft at Cards (a diverfion which fhe affected not, but to comply with others, when fometymes fhe could not avoid it). Behold, Madam, with what remorfe, with what difcretion.

" June the 2d.
" I will never play this halfe year butt att 3 penny omber, and then with one att halves. I will not; I doe not vow, but I will not doe it,—what, loofe mony att Cards, yett not give the poore? 'Tis robbing God, miffpending tyme, and miffimploying my Talent: three great Sinns. Three pounds would have kept three people from ftarveing a month: well, I will not play."

Here is a bleffed Creature. 'Tis in this pretious Manufcript that I find an account of the particular mercyes fhe

fhe had received from God, amongft
which that he had given foe religious a
Mother, fuch good breeding, early receiveing the blefled facrament, the
prayers of holy people for her, and
afliftance of a fpirittuall Guide, which
(fayes fhe) I am confident was the reward of my receiveing at the Charter
houfe. I take notice of it here, becaufe
'tis there fhe blefled God that fhe had
been ferviceable, both to poore and
Rich, in that he had been pleafed to
make her his Inftrument, and foe goes
on to thank him for the many perfonall
dangers and accidents fhe had efcaped,
all which fhe particularizes. But to
returne to her Charityes, (than which
I know no greater marke of a confummate Chriftian,) I may not omit that
other branch of it, her vifitting and re-
leafeing of prifoners, of which I think
I can produce a lift of above thirty re-
ftrained for debts in feverall prifons,
which fhe paid and compounded for at
once.

once. Nor were thefe as (I faid) fudden fitts of devotion, but her continued practice, and fuch as tooke up a confiderable portion of her life; and fuch infinite fatisfaction tooke fhe in this bleffed Imployment, as that often have I knowne her privately flipp away and breake from the gay and publique Company, the greateft entertainments, and greateft perfons too of the Court, to make a ftepp to fome miferable poore fick Creature, whilft thofe fhe quitted have wondered why fhe went from the converfation; and more they would, had they feen how the fceene was chang'd from a Kingly palace to fome meane cottage, from the Company of princes to poore neceffitous wretches, when by and by fhe would returne as chearfull and in good humour, as if fhe had been about fome worldly concerne, and excufe her abfence in the moft innocent manner imaginable. Never muft I forgett the infinite pleafure fhe tooke in
doeing

F F

doeing Charityes. 'Twas one day that I was with her, when seeing a poore Creature in the streets, "Now," sayes she to me, "how will I make that miserable wretch rejoyce." Upon which she sent him ten tymes more than I am confident he ever could expect. This she spake, not as boasting, but soe as one might perceive her very soule lifted up in secret Joy, to consider how the miserable man would be made happy with the surprize. Soe as summing all these Instances together, I might well compare this Lady to those excellent persons whose praise is in the Gospell, and whose names (St. Paull assures us, Acts x. 2,) are written in the booke of life, being like Cornelius and Dorcas, full of good works and Almes Deeds which she did; as Priscilla, she instructed many more perfectly in the wayes of God; as Mary, she bestowed much labour; nor doe I ever think of her but I call to mind the

Phebes,

Phebes, and Triphofas, Julia and Olympia, Claudia and to whome the Appoftle would certainly have added Margarita, (this pearle of ours,) had fhe been then in the world, who were fervants of the Churches, fuccourers of the Saints, helpers in Chrift Jefus, and who were even ready to lay downe their lives for the Gofpell. Soe flagrant was her zeale, foe pure her Charitye, foe vehement and fincere her love to God, as often to quitt the Eafe and pleafures of life, and difmifs the Diverfions of a Court, to poffefs thofe Divine and fupernall pleafures of doeing good, and the bleffing of him that was ready to perifh came upon her who caufed the widows heart to fing for Joy, for fhe was Eyes to the blind, and feet to the Lame, in all things, fhewing herfelfe a patterne of good workes. In a word, her life did foe fhine before Men, that thofe who faw her good workes could not butt be ftirred up to glorifye God; yet by

grace

grace we are faved through faith, and not of our felves, it is the gift of God, not of workes, left any man fhould boaft, for we are his workmanfhip, created in Chrift Jefus unto good workes, which God hath before ordained that we fhould walke in them.

And now after all this, I need noe more produce her Diarye, haveing given your Ladyfhipp fo minute an Account of her life and actions, I fhall onely add, that to the particulars of the Mercyes fhe received, Refolutions made, and Graces which fhe defired, fhe compofed many excellent Prayers, Praifes, and Devotions, pertinent to the occafion, and to which I might fubjoine the wonderfull Condefcenfion, already noted, in conftantly giveing me once a year a little hiftory of her life, and what had happened of moft concerne in her particular, what faileings, and Improvements fhe was fencible of, with an Ingenuitye

genuitye exterordnary, and breathing
a pious friendſhipp, deſireing my direction and my prayers, which a thou-
ſand tymes I needed more than ſhe,
who had, (as your Ladyſhipp well
knows, and is already noted) a Ghoſtly
father, with whome frequently corre-
ſponding, ſhe conſtantly received proper
Miniſteryes and advice in matters cog-
nizable to that ſacred Character. To
him it was ſhe often revealed her Conſcience, as from a Child ſhe before had
done to a devout and learned prelate of
our Church by the exterordnary Care
of his [her ?] pious and excellent Mother, as herſelf has told me, lookeing
on it as the greateſt bleſſing ſhe had
ever left her.

And thus, Madam, I have, according to the beſt of my poore ability,
complyed with your Ladyſhipp's comands, and given you the Life of this
Incomparable Lady : which though I
may

may not have performed to the height and merit of the fubject, I have yet me-thinks paid an obligation to the memory of one you loved, and that honoured me with friendfhip never to be forgotten, fince it let me into a Converfation of foe great advantage. In a word, to juftifye what I prefent your Ladyfhipp, and fumm up all. I have been oft partaker of her fadnefs and brighter dayes, wittnefs of her devouteft Recollections, accurate and exterordinary preparations, ardent Zeale, and unwearyed Devotions, chearfull and even profufive Charityes and labours of Love, for her fecular concerns was only in order to Spirittuall.

In fumme.

Never was there a more unfpotted virgin, a more loyall wife, a more fincere friend, a more confummate Chriftian ; add

add to this, a florid youth, an exquifite and naturall beauty, and gracefull-
nefs the moft becomeing. Nor was fhe
to be difguifed : there was nothing
more quick and peircing than her apprehenfion, nothing more faithfull than
her memory, more folid and mature
than her Judgment, infomuch as I
have heard her hufband affirme to me
(whofe difcernment all that have the
honour to know him will allow to be
exterordinary) that even in the greateft
difficultyes and occafions, he has both
afked and preferred her advice with
continuall fuccefs, and with thefe folid
parts fhe had all the advantages of a
moft fparkling witt, a naturall Eloquence, a gentle and agreeable tone of
voice, and a charmeing accent when
fhe fpake, whilft the Charmes of her
countenance were made up of the greateft Innocence, modefty, and goodnefs
Imaginable, agreeable to the Compo-
fure of her thoughts, and the union of
                              a thou-

a thoufand perfections : add to all this,
fhe was Juft, Invincible, fecrett, ingeni-
oufly finceere, faithfull in her promifes,
and to a Miracle, temperate, and miftrefs of her paffions and refolutions, and
foe well had fhe imployed her fpann of
tyme, that as oft as I confider how
much fhe knew, and writt, and did, I
am plainly aftonifhed, and blufh even
for my felfe.   O how delightfull entertaining was this Lady, how grave
her difcourfe, how unlike the Converfation of her fex, when fhe was the moft
facetious, it would allwayes end in a
chearfull compofednefs the moft becomeing in the world, for fhe was the
tendereft Creature living of taking
advantage of anothers Imperfections ;
nothing could be more humble and full
of Compaffion, nothing more difpofed
to all offices of kindnefs.   In a word,
what perfections were fcatered amongft
others of her fex, feem'd here to be
united, and fhe went every day im-
                              proveing,

proveing, fhineing brighter and afcend-
ing ftill in vertue.

I fhould here add fomething concerning the obfequies and funerall of
this bleffed Saint, on which occafion is
not to be omitted, the earneft requeft
fhe foe provifionally made, that fhe
might be interred in the Dormitorye
of her hufband's family and Relations,
tho' it were not much lefs then three
hundred miles diftance from the place
where fhe was borne and bred, that
foe her afhes might hereafter be mingl'd with his whome foe intirely fhe
loved ; and which, after her Corps had
been embalm'd and wrapt in Lead, was
(as your Ladyfhipp knows) as religioufly perform'd, decently and with
much honour, but without pomp or
oftentation, on the 16th day of September, 1678, in the Church of Bre-
ague, in the parifh of Godolphin, in
Cornwall, of which that family have
been

been Lords and of illuftrious name both
before and fince the Conqueft; and
where, being alive, fhe had often in my
hearing expreffed fuch a longing defire
to have paffed the reft of her dayes,
that, being remote from the noife of
Cittyes, Courts, and the fubjecting Im-
pertinences attending them, fhe might
intirely vacate [to] the fervice of God: not
but that wherever fhe lived fhe did it as
much as ever any bleffed Creature did,
but becaufe fhe fancyed fhe fhould doe
it better there, which was impoffible.

Here then let us leave our Saint at
reft, but our felves at none, till by following her example wee arrive at that
bleffed repofe whether fhe is gone before.

For thou (deare Soule) to Heavens fledd,
Haft all the vertues with thee, thither
    Wee here fee thee no more. [*ledd,*
Thou to that bright and glorious place
              Art

Art runn, haſt won the Race:
 A Crowne of Rayes,
 And never fadeing Bayes,
Such as on Heaven's Parnaſſus grows,
 Deck thyne Angelick Brows;
A Robe of Righteouſneſs about thee caſt.
Bathed in Celeſtiall Bliſs, thou there doſt
  taſt
 Pleaſures att God's right hand,
 Pleaſures that ever laſt,
And greater then wee here can vnder-
  ſtand,
Butt are for ſuch as ſerve him beſt re-
  ſerv'd in ſtore.

   2.

How long, Lord, ah! how long
 Wate wee below!
Our ſoden feete ſtick in the Clay,
Wee thro' the bodye's Dungeon ſee no day.
 Sorrows on ſorrows throng,
Friendſhipps (the ſouls of life) and
  frends depart
To other worlds, and new Relations know.
     Ah!

Ah! thou who art
The ſtarry orbs above
Eſſentiall love,
Reach forth thy gratious hand,
And ſend me wings for flight,
Sett me vpon that holy Land,
O bring me to the happy ſhoare
Where no dark night
Obſcure the day, where all is light;
A Citty there not made with hands
Within the bliſsfull Region ſtands,
Where wee in every ſtreete
Our deareſt friends againe ſhall meete,
And friendſhipps more refin'd and ſweete,
And never looſe them more.
Amen.

FINIS.

Epitaph.

Epitaph.

In Margaritam Epitaphium.

*Here lyes a pearle none such the ocean
    yields
In all the Treasures of his liquid fields ;
Butt such as that wise Merchant wisely
    sought
Who the bright Gemm with all his sub-
    stance bought.
Such to Jerusalem above translates
Our God, t'adorne the Entrance of her
    gates.
The Spouse with such Embrodery does
    come
To meete her Nuptialls the Celestiall
    Groome.*

On the copper plate sothered
on the Coffinn.

Notes.

Page 1.

 ADY SYLVIUS. Anne, daughter of William Howard, fourth fon of Thomas, firft Earl of Berkfhire, and wife of Sir Gabriel Sylvius. See Table IV.

P. 5. " *An ancient Suffolke family.*" See Table I. and the note attached to it.

P. 6. " *Mrs. Blagge.*" See the fame table.

P. 7. " *Bifhop of Ely.*" Dr. Peter Gunning, Bifhop of Chichefter in 1669, Bifhop of Ely in 1674, who "can do nothing but what is well."—*Diary*, Feb. 23, 1673.

P. 8. " *Old Duchefs of Richmond.*" Mary Villiers, fifter of George, fecond Duke of Buckingham, and widow of James Stuart, third Duke of Richmond. See Table III.

P. 8. " *late Countefs of Guilford.*" Elizabeth Fielding, coufin of the Duke of Buckingham

ham and of the Duchefs of Richmond.   See
Table III.

P. 8.   *" Groom of the Stoole,"* (Cuſtos Stolæ.)
The Countefs of Guilford was ſucceeded, as
" groom of the ſtole" to Henrietta Maria, by
Lady Arlington (Iſabella de Naſſau, who afterwards married Henry Fitzroy, firſt Duke of Graf-
ton).   At a later period, in 1704, the Duchefs of
Marlborough was appointed " Groom of the
Stole" to Queen Anne, but the title of her office
was changed to " Miſtrefs of the Robes."   Elizabeth, the heirefs of the great houfe of Percy and
wife of Charles, (the proud) Duke of Somerſet,
was made " Groom of the Stole" in 1710.   Since
the acceſſion of the Houfe of Hanover, the title
of " Groom of the Stole," has been given, I believe, excluſively, to the principal noble attendant
on the perfon of the King, and now, of the Prince
Confort.   In p. 103 Lord Rocheſter is called
Maſter of the Robes, and Godolphin himſelf was
appointed to that office in July 1678.   In ſome
French memoirs the title has been ſpelled "Grum-
ftul," and a ſingular perverſion of its meaning may
be ſeen in the Memoirs of the Comte de Brienne.

P. 8.   *" the late Queen's mother."*   An error
for *Queen-mother :* viz. Henrietta Maria, who
died Aug. 10. 1669.

P. 9.   *" the then Duchefs of York."*   Anne
Hyde, daughter of the Lord Chancellor Clarendon,

don, and firſt wife of James, Duke of York, afterwards James II.

P. 11. *" till the Duchefs died."* March 31,
1671.

P. 12. *" My Lady Falmouth."* Elizabeth
(or Mary ?) Bagot, daughter of Hervey Bagot,
who had been one of the maids of honour to the
Duchefs of York, and who was at this time the
widow of Charles Berkeley, firſt Vifcount Fitz-
hardinge and Earl of Falmouth, killed in the fea-
fight with the Dutch, June 3, 1665. Pepys calls
her, in 1666, " a pretty woman; ſhe was now
in her fecond or third mourning, and pretty pleafant in her looks." In July 1667, he fays that
ſhe was about to marry young Jermyn : ſhe however married, for her fecond huſband, Charles
Sackville, Earl (afterwards created Duke) of Dorfet. See Table II.

P. 21. *" Some play to be acted by the maids
of honour."* See an account of what took place
on Dec. 15, 1674.

P. 21. *" Duchefs of Monmouth."* The Lady
Anne Scot, daughter and fole heir of Francis,
Earl of Buccleuch, wife of James, Duke of Mon-
mouth, who was beheaded July 15, 1685.

P. 22. *" That of Micha,"* rather Malachi
iii. 17.

P. 27. *" Our familyes being neare to one another."* The family feat of the Evelyns was at
Wotton,

Wotton, in Surrey, where Evelyn often vifited, although he did not refide there till May 1694. Afhted, near Epfom, belonged to Sir Robert Howard, uncle to Lady Sylvius : Deepden, now Mr. Hope's, belonged to Mr. Charles Howard, anceftor of the prefent Duke of Norfolk : and Albury, now Mr. Drummond's, was the refidence of Henry Howard, afterwards Duke of Norfolk. All thefe places are at fhort diftances from each other.

P. 27. " *Your mother and fifter.*" Mrs. William Howard, [Elizabeth, daughter of Lord Dundas] and Dorothy Howard, afterwards Mrs. Graham. See Table IV.

P. 30. " *Your fifter, then maid of honour.*" See the laft note.

P. 34. " *Paulina and Euftochius.*" See p. 62, and all the accounts of St. Jerome.

P. 48. " *Att Whitehall, whither fhe came from St. James,*" to the Queen's fervice, after the death of the Duchefs of York in 1671.

P. 52. " *Mr. Godolphin fent abroad.*" In 1668 he accompanied his brother Sir William on a miffion to Spain.

P. 56. " *At Berkley houfe.*" The fplendid manfion built by Sir John Berkeley of Bruton, created Lord Berkeley of Stratton, at Hay Hill Farm, in the parifh of St. James. The names and titles are ftill preferved in *John* Street, *Berke-ley*

ley Square and Street, *Bruton* Street, *Stratton* Street, *Hay* Street, *Hill* Street and alfo *Hay-hill*, *Farm* Street, and *Charles* Street, after Lord Berkeley's brother, Charles, Earl of Falmouth. Part of the gardens are ftill preferved in thofe attached to Devonfhire Houfe and Lanfdowne (originally Bute) Houfe. Some idea of their extent may be formed from this enumeration. A defcription of Berkeley Houfe is given by Evelyn in his Diary, Sept. 25, 1672: no view of it is known to exift. Pennant, whofe error is copied by many others, ftrangely attributes the building of this houfe to the family of the *Earls of Berkeley*: of courfe the fcandalous anecdote introduced by him is equally out of place with his more fober narrative that Chriftian, Countefs of Devonfhire, lived " in the antient houfe—on the fite of Berkeley Houfe, where fhe received Waller and Denham, and where fhe died in 1674," (Jan. 16, 1674-5). Now John, Lord Berkeley of Stratton, the builder of Berkeley Houfe, did not die till the year 1678, and, after his death, his widow continued to refide there; for in 1684, Evelyn was confulted by Lady Berkeley of Stratton as to the propriety of building two ftreets in Berkeley Gardens, " referving the houfe and as much of the gardens as the breadth of the houfe," apparently Berkeley Street and Stratton Street. After the death of Lady Berkeley, the manfion was inhabited

bited by the Princefs (afterwards Queen) Anne
until Jan. 1695.

The old town houfe of the Earls of Devonfhire was not in Piccadilly, but in Bifhopfgate,
where Devonfhire Square now ftands; William,
the fecond earl, died there in 1628. His widow,
Chriftian, the loyal and exemplary Countefs of
Devonfhire, did not refide in London, fhe lived
and died at Roehampton in Surrey, in the houfe
which had been inhabited by Wefton, Earl of
Portland, and now belongs to Mr. Robert Gofling the banker. It was at Roehampton, not in
Piccadilly, that fhe received Waller and Denham.
Her fon William, the third earl, died in the fame
houfe in Nov. 1684. His fon William, the
fourth Earl (afterwards created Duke) of Devonfhire, having, at firft, no town houfe, rented
and lived in Montague Houfe (the Britifh Mufeum in Great Ruffell Street), which was burned
down during his occupation of it in Jan. 1686.
After the acceffion of William III. " the Duke of
Devonfhire took it into his head, that could he
have the Duchefs of Portfmouth's lodgings (at
Whitehall) where there was a fine room for
balls, it would give him a very magnificent air."
(Duchefs of Marlborough's Defence of her Conduct, p. 29.) It is probable that the Duke pur-
chafed Berkeley Houfe after 1695, and changed
its name to Devonfhire Houfe, fince Bifhop Ken-
net

net fays he died Aug. 18, 1707, in "Devonfhire Houfe, *Piccadilly.*" The prefent Devonfhire Houfe, ftanding certainly on the fite of Berkeley Houfe, was not built by him, but by his grandfon, the third duke, fome time after the year 1730. To this houfe and to its builder applies the epigram compofed by Horace (afterwards Lord Walpole of Wolterton), brother of Sir Robert Walpole, who, calling one day at Devonfhire Houfe, which was juft finifhed, and not finding the Duke at home, left this epigram upon the table,

"Ut dominus, domus eft; non extra fulta columnis
Marmoreis fplendet; quod tenet, intus habet."

Sir John Denham, whofe name being affociated with that of the Countefs of Devonfhire perhaps mifled Pennant, had a houfe and gardens in Piccadilly, where Burlington Houfe now ftands, adjoining to which ftood Lord Clarendon's famous manfion, afterwards the Duke of Albemarle's, the fite of the prefent Albemarle Street, Dover Street, and Bond Street. The three manfions thus named, viz. Sir John Denham's, Albemarle Houfe, and Berkeley Houfe, occupied nearly the whole of the north of Piccadilly : the ground to the weft of Berkeley Houfe was divided into fix fields, known as "Pennilefs Bank," "Little Brook-field," "Stone Bridge-field," "Great Brook-field," "Mr. Audley's land," and "Shoulder of Mutton Field." To the north, Berkeley Gardens were

were bounded by the land "where graze the cows" of Alexander Davies, of Ebury, in Pimlico, whose daughter and heir, Mary, married Sir Thomas Grosvenor in 1676, and whose name is preserved in "Davies Street."

George, Lord Berkeley, of Berkeley, afterwards Earl of Berkeley, lived at another Berkeley House, in the parish of St. John's, Clerkenwell, on the site of the present Berkeley Street, which leads from St. John's Lane to Red Lion Street. His family had lived there for several generations, his father died there Aug. 1658, his third son James was baptized there, 1 June 1663, and from the same house he writes on Feb. 23, 1678, to Pepys, who on the previous day acknowledges a letter from his lordship "*at St. John's*" (Correspondence, vol. v. pp. 42 — 45). In Clerkenwell also, in 1681, Lord Berkeley received a deputation (headed by Tillotson, then Dean of Canterbury) from Sion College, to which he had presented the library collected by Sir Robert Coke, son of Lord Chief Justice Coke. From the Coke family Lord Berkeley inherited Durdans, near Epsom, mentioned as his residence both by Evelyn and Pepys. Clerkenwell has long since ceased to be a fashionable neighbourhood, but in the seventeenth century it possessed the mansions of the Earls of Aylesbury, Berkeley, and Northampton, the Duke of Newcastle, the Challoner family, &c. : Bishop Burnet
and

and many others attached to the court alſo reſided there. The ſtreets are many of them named after their former owners or inhabitants. The Marquis of Northampton ſtill retains vaſt property in Clerkenwell and Iſlington.

P. 60. *"The mother of the maids."* Lady Sanderſon, wife of Sir William Sanderſon.

P. 61. *"My Lady."* Lady Berkeley (ſee Table II.) was Chriſtiana, daughter of Sir Andrew Riccard, Knight; and widow of Henry Rich, Lord Kenſington, only ſon of Robert Rich, ſecond Earl of Holland and fifth Earl of Warwick, by Elizabeth Ingram, his firſt wife. Sir Andrew Riccard was one of London's richeſt merchant-princes: he was Preſident of the Eaſt India Company, and in that capacity figures in the great caſe of monopolies, Skinner *v.* E. I. Company. A marble ſtatue, erected to his honour by the Turkey Company, of which he was preſident for eighteen years, ſtill exiſts on his monument in the Church of St. Olave, Hart Street. He was knighted July 10, 1668, and died Sept. 6, 1672, aged 68.

P. 61. *"Your two ſiſters."* Apparently an error for *"you* two ſiſters." See Table IV.

P. 67. *"Her ſiſter, the Lady Yarborough."* See Table I. It may ſuffice here to ſtate that this lady, [Henrietta Maria Blagge] whoſe conduct was not free from blame, has been miſtaken by ſome fome editors of Grammont and by Horace Walpole for the fubject of this memoir.

P. 67. *"The Dean of Hereford."* George Benfon.

P. 84. *"From Twicknam."* "Twickenham Park, Lord Berkeley's country feat," Diary, March 23, 1676. It was lately the property of Mr. Francis Gofling, the banker.

P. 93. *"Play at Court before their Majefties."* "Saw a comedie at night at Court, acted by the ladies only, amongft them Lady Mary and Ann, his Royal Highnefs' two daughters, and my dear friend Mrs. Blagg, who having the principal part, performed it to admiration. They were all covered with jewels," Diary, Dec. 15, 1674. The play was "Califto or the Chafte Nymph," by John Crowne. It was printed in 1675, and a copy is preferved in the library of the Britifh Mufeum. After the title-page is a lift of the performers, all of whom however did not bear, at the time of acting the play, the titles which the printed lift gives to them. The lift is as follows:

Califto, a chafte and favourite nymph of Diana, beloved by Jupiter. "Her Highnefs the Lady Mary," a daughter of the Duke of York, and afterwards Queen of England.

Nyphe, a chafte young nymph, friend to Califto. "Her Highnefs the Lady Anne," a daughter

ter of the Duke of York, and afterwards Queen
of England.

Jupiter, in love with Califto. "The Lady
Henrietta Wentworth," rather Henrietta, Baron-
efs Wentworth, which dignity defcended to her
on the death, in 1665, of her father, Thomas
Wentworth, laft Earl of Cleveland. She is well
known from her difgraceful connexion at a later
period with the Duke of Monmouth, whom fhe
did not long furvive, dying on April 23, 1686.

Juno. "The Countefs of Suffex." Lady Anne
Fitzroy, daughter of Charles II. by the Duchefs
of Cleveland and wife of Thomas, Lord Dacre and
Earl of Suffex.

Pfecas, an envious nymph, enemy to Califto,
beloved by Mercury. "The Lady Mary Mordant," daughter and heir of Henry, fecond Earl
of Peterborough: fhe married in 1677, Henry,
feventh Duke of Norfolk, from whom fhe was
divorced in April 1700. She afterwards married
Sir John Germaine, to whom fhe left a great part
of the Peterborough eftates.

Diana, goddefs of Chaftity. "Mrs. Blagge,
late maid of honour to the Queen." Mrs. Go-
DOLPHIN.

Mercury, in love with *Pfecas*. "Mrs. Jennings, maid of honour to the Duchefs." Sarah
Jennings, afterwards married to John Churchill,
the great Duke of Marlborough.

The

The " Nymphs attending on Diana, who alfo danced in the Prologue, and in feveral Entries in the Play," were

"The Countefs of Darby." Dorothea Helena, daughter of John Poliander de Kirkhoven, by Catharine, Countefs of Chefterfield, daughter of Thomas, fecond Lord Wotton. The Countefs was widow of Charles Stanley, eighth Earl of Derby, who had died Dec. 21, 1672.

"The Countefs of Pembroke." Henriette de Querouaille (fifter to the Duchefs of Portfmouth), wife of Philip Herbert, feventh Earl of Pembroke. Bifhop Kennett fpells the name *Carewell.*

"The Lady Katharine Herbert." Sifter-in-law to the preceding, being daughter of Philip, fifth Earl of Pembroke, by Katharine, daughter of Sir William Villiers of Brookefby.

" Mrs. Fitz-Gerald." Probably Katharine (daughter of John Fitz Gerald of Dromana), who married in 1677, Edward Villiers, eldeft fon of George, fourth Vifcount Grandifon.

" Mrs. Frazier, maid of honour to the Queen."

The " men that danced" were

" His Grace the Duke of Monmouth."

"The Vifcount Dunblaine." Edward Of-borne, Lord Latimer, one of the Gentlemen of the Bedchamber to Charles II., eldeft fon of Thomas, Earl of Danby (afterwards created Marquis of Carmarthen and Duke of Leeds). After the representation, reprefentation, but before the publication of the piece, the Earl of Danby was created Vifcount Dunblaine in Scotland, which dignity was affumed as a title of courtefy by his fon, Lord Latimer. By Table I. it will be feen that the prefent Duke of Leeds is the lineal reprefentative of Mrs. Godolphin.

"The Lord Daincourt." Robert Leake, eldeft fon of Nicolas, fecond Earl of Scarfdale, whom he afterwards fucceeded in that title.

"Mrs. Moon."

"Mr. Harpe."

"Mr. Lane."

Neither in this lift, nor amongft the names given in the Diary, is the name of the Duchefs of Monmouth, whom Evelyn here mentions as one of "the fhineing beautyes" who performed. It is probable that Evelyn's Diary written at the time, corroborated as it is by the publifhed lift, is the more correct on this point. The Duchefs of Monmouth too had fome years before met with a fevere accident whilft dancing, which caufed an incurable lamenefs. See Pepys' Diary, Sept. 20, 1668.

P. 100. "*The Countefs of Suffolk.*" "Was at the repetition of the paftoral, on which occafion Mrs. Blagg had about her neere 20,000*l.* worth of Jewells, of which fhe loft one, worth about 80*l.*, borrow'd of the Countefs of Suffolk. The prefs was fo greate, that 'tis a wonder fhe loft

no

no more: The Duke made it good." Diary, Dec.
22, 1674. The Countefs of Suffolk was Barbara,
daughter of Sir Edward Villiers, (fee Table III.)
widow of Sir Richard Wentworth, and fecond
wife of James Howard, third Earl of Suffolk. She
died in 1681.

P. 103. " *The mafter of the Robes, now Earle
of Rochefter.*" Laurence Hyde (fecond fon of
the Chancellor Clarendon) created Earl of Rochefter at the end of 1682, a fact which proves
that Evelyn did not write this life until fome
years after Mrs. Godolphin's death.

P. 103. " *Dr. Lake.*" John Lake, afterwards Bifhop of Chichefter.

P. 107. " *My lady Hamilton.*" " A fprightly
young lady, much in the good graces of the
[Berkeley] family, wife of that valiant and worthy
gentleman George Hamilton, not long after flain
in the wars. She had been a maid of honour to
the Duchefs and now turned Papift." Diary, 12
Nov. 1675. This was Frances Jennings (elder
fifter of Sarah, Duchefs of Marlborough) widow
of Sir George Hamilton, grandfon of James, firft
Earl of Abercorn, and brother of Count Anthony
Hamilton, author of the Memoires de Grammont.
Lady Hamilton afterwards married Richard Talbot, created Duke of Tyrconnel, and is well known
as the Duchefs of Tyrconnel. After this it is
curious to read in Pennant's words, " Above ftairs
(at

(at the New Exchange in the Strand) fat, in the character of a millener, the reduced Duchefs of Tyrconnel, wife to Richard Talbot, lord deputy of Ireland under James II. a bigoted papift, and fit inftrument of the defigns of the infatuated prince, who had created him Earl before his abdication, and after that, Duke of Tyrconnel. A female, fufpected to have been his duchefs, after his death, fupported herfelf for a few days (till fhe was known and otherwife provided for) by the little trade of this place: having delicacy enough not to wifh to be detected, fhe fat in a white mafk, and a white drefs, and was known by the name of the *white widow.*" This ftory, if true, forms a fingular contraft to that which Pepys relates of her in his Diary, 21 Feb. 1664-5, "What mad freaks the mayds of honor at court have! that Mrs. Jenings, one of the Dutcheffe's maids, the other day dreffed herfelf like an orange wench, and went up and down and cried oranges; till falling down, or by fome accident, her fine fhoes were difcerned, and fhe put to a great deal of fhame." The Duchefs of Tyrconnel died in Dublin 7 March, 1730; her hufband died Aug. 14, 1691.

P. 109. "*Ambaffador to the Court of France.*" John, Lord Berkeley, of Stratton, (fee Table II.) left England on this Embaffy 14 Nov. 1675. Evelyn in his Diary for Oct. and Nov. in 1675, gives

gives many particulars. If we were to truſt to
the editor of Evelyn's Diary and to the noble
editor of Pepys', the Lord and Lady Berkeley, ſo
often named as Mrs. Godolphin's warm friends,
were George Lord Berkeley, afterwards created
Earl of Berkeley, and his wife Elizabeth, daughter and co-heir of John Maſſingbeard, eſq. of Lin-
colnſhire, and in the abſence of all connexion
between them and the families of Blagge and Godolphin there would be great difficulty in ſhowing
any probable cauſe for the friendſhip, not to call
it patronage, which Mrs. Godolphin and her huſband received. The editors of Evelyn and Pepys
have unfortunately fallen into the error, which I
have pointed out as having been committed before
them by Pennant, of confounding the two Lords
Berkeley, if not the two " Berkeley-houſes."

Lord Berkeley *of Stratton* originally known
as Sir John Berkeley, and in the ſervice of Charles
I. at the ſame time with Colonel Blagge, Mrs.
Godolphin's father, was concerned with John
Aſhburnham and Colonel Legge in the flight of
Charles I. from Hampton Court to the Iſle of
Wight, a vexed point of hiſtory, on which Lord
Clarendon's misſtatements have been well cor-
rected by the late Earl of Aſhburnham: During
the exile of the royal family he became the
favourite of James, Duke of York, whoſe fa-
vour he never loſt; although he was repreſented

to

to Charles as the fecret agent of the Court of
France, and as the known enemy of the Chancellor Clarendon and his party. The Chancellor's
enmity Berkeley fhared alike with Afhburnham
and Legge, the firft however obtained his peerage
in 1658, as the price of James' return to his brother Charles; the others, although high in favour
with Charles II. were ennobled in the perfons of
their defcendants. Clarendon makes the enmity
between himfelf and Berkeley to arife from his
oppofition to Berkeley's claim to the mafterfhip of
the Court of Wards: James II. in his Memoirs,
from Clarendon's advice to Lady Morton to rejeft
Berkeley's propofals of marriage. Lady Morton,
one of the brighteft ornaments of " the beautiful
race of·Villiers," was Elizabeth, daughter of Sir
Edward Villiers, niece of the Duke of Buckingham, and widow of Robert Douglas, 8th Earl of
Morton, who died in 1649. Whilft Lady Dal-
keith, and during the ftay of Charles the Firft's
family at Exeter, fhe had had the charge of the
Princefs Henrietta, afterwards Duchefs of Or-
leans, and to her Fuller infcribes his " Good
Thoughts in Bad Times." Her noble refcue of
her royal ward, whom fhe carried on her back to
Dover, in the difguife of a beggar and her child,
is well known. Lady Morton died in 1654.
Befides enjoying the perfonal favour of the Duke
of York, Berkeley was a near kinfman of the in-
fluential

fluential Harry Jermyn, Earl of St. Alban's, who, as we fee by the table of the Blagge family, was alfo a relative of Mrs. Godolphin: the clofe connexion of the Berkeley and Godolphin families fully accounts for the long and intimate friendfhip which exifted between them.

After the Reftoration Berkeley's rife was rapid, and his employments numerous. In 1660 he wa appointed a commiffioner of the Admiralty, in June 1662 a privy counfellor for Ireland, and foon afterwards Lord Prefident of Connaught. In 1664 he was made a mafter of the ordnance, and in 1665 a commiffioner of Tangier. All thefe offices he held at the fame time, and fo early as 1663, Pepys fays that Lord Berkeley boafted of having gained £50,000 in the navy alone. This fum appears fo great that I fufpeft fome error in the tranfcription of Pepys' Diary. If it be true, there can be no wonder that, in 1665, we read of Berkeley's beginning a houfe at St. James', next to the Lord Chancellor's, nor at Evelyn's mentioning, in 1672, that it had coft £30,000. He had alfo more indireft ways of obtaining money through his influence with the Duke of York, as Pepys mentions in 1668. In April 1670 Lord Berkeley was appointed Lord Lieutenant of Ireland, where he remained till Auguft 1672. In October 1674, he was named to the embaffy to France, in which he was accompanied by Mrs. Godolphin

Godolphin and by Evelyn's fon. From this embaffy he returned in June 1677, and in the following year he died.

As Evelyn and Pepys' Diaries may be confulted, I add the following corrected index to the
places where Lord Berkeley *of Stratton* is meant,
(8vo. editions). Evelyn ii. 255. 260. 373-375.
398. 413. 417. 421. 425. iii. 90. 117. 177. 338.
Pepys i. 115. 121. 122. 163. 282.; ii. 21. 101.
132. 141. 173. 224. 238. 249, 250. 256. 346.
423.; iii. 167. 183. 228. 236. 386. 395.; iv.
62. 174. 181. The other places relate to George,
Lord Berkeley, of Berkeley, afterwards Earl of
Berkeley, viz. Evelyn, vol. ii. 136. 140. 147.
198. 214. 385.; vol. iii. 67. Pepys, vol. i. 39.
95. 305.; vol. ii. 80.; vol. iii. 87. 230. 291.
vol. v. 42-45.

P. 120. " *Nothing like Pinto's Travels.*"
The name of Fernam Mendez Pinto will ever
remain affociated with falfehood and exaggeration.
He lived in the 16th century, but his travels
were not tranflated into Englifh until 1663,
whence probably Mrs. Godolphin's acquaintance
with them. Congreve's well known lines, almoft
become proverbial, (and which it is impoffible to
quote without remembering their witty applica-
tion by the prefent Bifhop of Llandaff,)

> " Fernam Mendez Pinto was but a type of thee,
> Thou liar of the firft magnitude ! "
> *Love for Love,* Act ii. Sc. 5.

were

were not written until after Mrs. Godolphin's death. Claude's *Défence de la Réformation*, written in reply to the Janfenift Nicole, was firft publifhed in 1673, fo that at the time of Mrs. Godolphin's vifit to Paris, the book muft have had the additional charm of novelty.

P. 121. " *That baile of theirs.*" Perhaps for *bale*, forrow, or deftruction.

P. 121. " *My charge your fon.*" " I fettled affaires, my fonn being to go into France, with my Lord Berkeley, defigned ambaffador extraordinary for France, and plenipotentiary for the general peace of Nimeguen." Diary, 15 Oct. 1675. This fon was John Evelyn, great-grandfather of the prefent Archbifhop of York. At this time he was about nineteen years of age.

P. 122. " *My Lady H.*" Lady Hamilton, fee p. 107.

P. 125. " *Mr. Bernard Greenvile,*" of Abf-Court at Walton on Thames in Surrey, " an old houfe in a pretty parke." Diary, 17 Sept. 1673. In Auguft 1672, Bernard Grenville had been fent on a miffion to Savoy, and it was probably on his return from this miffion that he efcorted Mrs. Godolphin to England. He was the fecond fon of Sir Beville Grenville, killed at Lanfdowne fight, whofe eldeft fon, Sir John Grenville, the bearer of Charles II.'s meffages to the Lords and Commons, was created Vifcount Lanfdowne and

Earl

Earl of Bath. After the death, without iſſue, of William, grandſon of the firſt Earl of Bath; George, ſecond ſon of Bernard Grenville, was created Lord Lanſdowne in 1711. He is well known from his poetical talents.

P. 126. *" Dr. Warnett's in Covent Garden, whoſe wife was her near relation."* Of this relationſhip I find no trace.

P. 129. *" Leaſe ſhe had of certaine lands in Spalding."* See Diary of 9 Nov. 1676. " Finiſhed the leaſe of Spalding for Mr. Godolphin."

P. 130. *" Her pretty habitation in Scotland Yard."* " To London, to take order about the building of an houſe, or rather an apartment which had all the conveniences of an houſe, for my deare friend Mr. Godolphin and lady, which I undertook to contrive and ſurvey, and employ workmen, till it ſhould be quite finiſhed, it being juſt over againſt his majeſties wood yard by the Thames ſide, leading to Scotland Yard." Diary, 12 Sept. 1676.

P. 136. *" The picture ſhe ſome years ſince beſtowed upon me."* See preface, and the portrait prefixed to this volume.

P. 137. *" My lady Viſcounteſs Mordant."* Elizabeth Carey, daughter and ſole heir of Thomas, ſecond ſon of Robert, Earl of Monmouth, wife of John, Viſcount Mordaunt of Avalon, eldeſt ſon of John, Earl of Peterborough.

P. 137.

P. 137. "*Your ladyſhip and ſiſter Gr*"(*aham*). Dorothy Howard, wife of Colonel James Graham of Levens.　See Table IV.

P. 138. "*Mr. Aſhmole's att Lambath.*"　This viſit was on the 23rd of July, and on the ſame day, "Mr. Godolphin was made maſter of the robes to the King."　On the 25 July, Evelyn adds, "there was ſent to me £70 from whom I knew not, to be by me diſtributed among poore people : I afterwards found it was from that deere friend (Mrs. Godolphin) who had frequently given me large ſums to beſtow on charities."　It is ſcarcely neceſſary to ſay that the muſeum called "Mr. Aſhmole's att Lambath" is now the Aſhmolean at Oxford.　Of the MSS. which Evelyn mentions in his Diary, a catalogue has recently been printed by the Univerſity.

P. 143. "*Mr. Harvye, treaſurer to her Majeſtye.*"　John Hervey, eldeſt ſon of Sir William Hervey of Ickworth; he was a great favourite with Charles II. a leading man in Parliament, and a patron of letters : he died 18 Jan. 1679.

P. 146. "*Dr. Needham.*"　Diary, Nov. 4, 1679.　"Went to the funerall of my pious, dear and ancient learned friend, Dr. Jaſper Needham, who was buried at St. Bride's Church.　He was a true and holy Chriſtian, and one who loved me with greate affection."

P. 146. "*Dr. Short.*"　Dr. Peregrine Short,
　　　　　　　　　　　　　　　　　　"reputed

" reputed a papift, but who was in truth, a very honeft good Chriftian," and by whofe advice Charles II. had firft taken the Jefuits back. Diary, 29 Nov. 1694.

P. 152. *" Mrs. Bofcawen,"* her fifter in law, fee Tables I. and V.

TABLE I.

TABLE I.

PEDIGREE OF BLAGGE AND GODOLPHIN.

Arg. 2 bends engrailed, gu. for BLAGGE.

CECILY, (*second wife*) dau. of Sir John Brooke, Lord Cobham, by Margaret, dau. of Edward Neville, Lord Abergavenny. She married also John Barret, and, thirdly, Sir Richard Walden, Knt. She died 35 Hen. VIII. = ROBERT BLAGGE, or BLAGUE, or BLAGE, co. Somerset, and Cleyndon, in Darent, co. Kent. Baron of the Exchequer, 27 June, 1511, d. 13 Sept. 1522. = KATHERINE, (*first wife*), dau. and h. of Thos. Brune, or Browne of Horseman's Place, in Dartford, co. Kent.

ANNE, (*first wife*) dau. of Sir George Hevening-ham. = SIR AMBROSE JERMYN, of Rushbrook, co. Suffolk, d. 1577. = DOROTHY, (*second wife*) dau. of William Badbye, widow of Richard Goodriche. In 1563, she had a lease from Eliz. of the manor of Stanmore, co. Middlesex. d. Apr. 1594. = SIR GEORGE BLAGGE, Knt. b. 1512, d. 1551. See note A. — BARNABY BLAGGE, who in 33 Hen. VIII. sold Horseman's Place, ob. s. p. — JOHN BLAGGE, s. p.

SIR ROBERT JERMYN, of Rushbrook, d. 19 April, 1614. = JUDITH BLAGGE, d. Oct. 1614. — HENRY BLAGGE, of Hornings-herth, co. Suffolk, who sold Cleyndon, 24 Eliz. d. Apr. 1596. = HESTHER JERMYN, m. 8 Oct. 1571. — CHARLES LE GRISE, of Brockdish. = HESTHER BLAGGE, m. 25 Nov. 1566.

SUSAN, who married Sir William Hervey, ancestor of the Marquess of Bristol. — SIR THOMAS JERMYN, of Rushbrooke, living 1622. = MARGARET CLARKE. — MARGARET = AMBROSE BLAGGE, of Horningsherth, d. 1662. = MARTHA BARBER, of Bury, *first wife,* m. 31 Mar. 1608, d. Aug. 1624. — DOROTHY BLAGGGE.

Five children.

THOMAS JERMYN, whose son, Thomas, succeeded as second Lord Jermyn, died s. p. in 1703. — HENRY JERMYN, created Lord Jermyn in 1684, with limitation to his brother, created Earl of St. Albans 1660. Died s. p. 1683. — COLONEL THOMAS BLAGGE, of Horningsherth, Groom of the Bedchamber to Charles I. and Governor of Wallingford, which surrendered to Fairfax in 1646. After the restoration he was colonel of a regiment and Governor of Yarmouth and Landguard Fort, d. 14 Nov. 1660, bur. at Westminster, where a monument to him formerly existed. = MARY NORTH, dau. of Sir Roger North, of Mildenhall, by Elizabeth, dau. of Sir John Gilbert, of Great Finborow, co. Suffolk. — GEORGE BLAGGE. HARRY BLAGGE. — MARTHA. JUDITH. ANNE. KATHARINE.

SIR THOMAS YARBURGH of Snaith, Sheriff of Yorksh. 1676, æt. 37. = HENRIETTA MARIA BLAGGE (for whom see Grammont's Memoirs). — DOROTHY BLAGGE. MARY BLAGGE. — MARGARET BLAGGE, b 2 Aug. 1652, Maid of Honor to Queen Catharine, m. 16 May, 1675, d. 9 Sept. 1678, buried at Breage, co. Cornwall, 16 Sept. 1678. = SIDNEY GODOLPHIN, 3rd son of Sir Francis Godolphin, K. B. A Lord of the Treasury in 1679, and First Lord in 1684. Created Lord Godolphin, *of Rialton,* in Sept. 1684. Lord High Treasurer in 1704, K. G. created Viscount Rialton, and Earl of Godolphin, 29 Dec. 1706. Died 1712. — HENRY GODOLPHIN, Provost of Eton, and Dean of St. Paul's, d. Jan. 1783. = MARY JANE dau. of Col. Sidney Godolphin. m. Edw. Boscawen, See Tab. V.

A   B   C

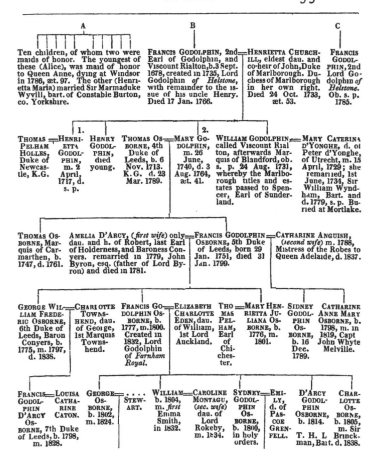

A

Ten children, of whom two were maids of honor. The youngest of these (Alice), was maid of honor to Queen Anne, dying at Windsor in 1786, æt. 97. The other (Henrietta Maria) married Sir Marmaduke Wyvill, bart. of Constable Burton, co. Yorkshire.

B

FRANCIS GODOLPHIN, 2nd=HENRIETTA CHURCHILL, eldest dau. and co-heir of John, Duke of Marlborough. Duchess of Marlborough in her own right. Died 24 Oct. 1733, æt. 53.

Earl of Godolphin, and Viscount Rialton, b. 3 Sept. 1678, created in 1735, Lord Godolphin *of Helstone*, with remainder to the issue of his uncle Henry. Died 17 Jan. 1766.

C

FRANCIS GODOLPHIN, 2nd Lord Godolphin *of Helstone*. Ob. s. p. 1785.

1.

THOMAS PELHAM HOLLES, Duke of Newcastle, K.G.=HENRIETTA GODOLPHIN, m. 2 April, 1717, d. s. p.

HENRY GODOLPHIN, died young.

THOMAS OSBORNE, 4th Duke of Leeds, b. 6 Nov. 1713. K.G. d. 23 Mar. 1789.=MARY GODOLPHIN, m. 26 June, 1740, d. 3 Aug. 1764, æt. 41.

2.

WILLIAM GODOLPHIN, called Viscount Rialton, afterwards Marquis of Blandford, ob. s. p. 24 Aug. 1731, whereby the Marlborough titles and estates passed to Spencer, Earl of Sunderland.

MARY CATERINA D'YONGHE, d. of Peter d'Yonghe, of Utrecht, m. 15 April, 1729; she remarried, 1st June, 1734, Sir William Wyndham, Bart. and d. 1779, s. p. Buried at Mortlake.

THOMAS OSBORNE, Marquis of Carmarthen, b. 1747, d. 1761.

AMELIA D'ARCY, (*first wife*) only dau. and h. of Robert, last Earl of Holderness, and Baroness Conyers. remarried in 1779, John Byron, esq. (father of Lord Byron) and died in 1781.=FRANCIS GODOLPHIN OSBORNE, 5th Duke of Leeds, born 29 Jan. 1751, died 31 Jan. 1799.=CATHARINE ANGUISH, (*second wife*) m. 1788, Mistress of the Robes to Queen Adelaide, d. 1837.

GEORGE WILLIAM FREDERIC OSBORNE, 6th Duke of Leeds, Baron Conyers, b. 1775, m. 1797, d. 1838.=CHARLOTTE TOWNSHEND, dau. of George, 1st Marquis Townshend.

FRANCIS GODOLPHIN OSBORNE, b. 1777, m. 1800. Created in 1832, Lord Godolphin of *Farnham Royal*.

ELIZABETH CHARLOTTE EDEN, dau. of William, 1st Lord Auckland.

THOMAS PELHAM, Earl of Chichester.=MARY HENRIETTA JULIANA OSBORNE, b. 1776, m. 1801.

SIDNEY GODOLPHIN OSBORNE, b. 16 Dec. 1789.

CATHARINE ANNE MARY OSBORNE, b. 1798, m. in 1819, Capt John Whyte Melville.

FRANCIS GODOLPHIN D'ARCY OSBORNE, 7th Duke of Leeds, b. 1798, m. 1828.=LOUISA CATHARINE CATON.

GEORGE OSBORNE, b. 1802, m. 1824.=.... STEWART.

WILLIAM, b. 1804, m. *first* Emma Smith, in 1832.=CAROLINE MONTAGU, (*sec. wife*) dau. of Lord Rokeby, m. 1834.

SYDNEY GODOLPHIN OSBORNE, b. 1800, in holy orders.=EMILY, d. of Pascoe GRENFELL.

D'ARCY GODOLPHIN OSBORNE, b. 1814.

CHARLOTTE OSBORNE, b. 1805, m. Sir T. H. L Brinckman, Bart. d. 1838.

NOTE A.

Notes.

Note A.

IR GEORGE BLAGGE deferves more notice than the mere mention of his name in the preceding table.

He was born in the year 1512, and was educated at Cambridge.[1] At a comparatively early age he was introduced at the Court of Henry VIII.[2] and in the abfence of other criteria we may judge favourably of him from the characters of his two chief companions and friends, the Earl of Surrey and Sir Thomas Wyat. In October, 1543, when the Imperialifts under the immediate eye of Charles V. aided by the Englifh under the command of Sir John Wallop, formed the fiege of Landreci,[3] which Francis I. haftened to relieve in perfon, Surrey with other young nobles, joined the Englifh forces, and was accompanied in his expedition by G. Blagge. Both incurred perfonal danger, and Sir John Wallop mentions in a letter to the King a narrow efcape of Blagge[4] in thefe terms. " Yefterday, Blagge, who arrived here with my Lord of Surrey, went with Mr. Carew to fee the faid trench, and efcaped very hardly from a piece of ordnance that was fhot towards him."

---

[1] Works of Surrey and Wyat, by Nott, vol. i. p. xcvi.
[2] Strype's Annals (Oxford Ed.), vol. ii. pt. ii. p. 419.
[3] Surrey and Wyat, vol. i. app. xxxix.
[4] Ib. vol. i. p. lvii.

A proof

A proof of the high eftimation in which Blagge was held by Surrey, is afforded by the following beautiful lines, prefixed to his verfion of the lxxiii Pfalm.[5]

> " *The fudden ftorms that heave me to and fro,*
>   *Had well near pierced Faith, my guiding fail.*
> *For I that on the noble voyage go*
>   *To fuccour truth, and falfehood to affail,*
> *Conftrained am to bear my fails full low ;*
>   *And never could attain fome pleafant gale.*
> *For unto fuch the profperous winds do blow*
>   *As men from port to port to feek avail.*
> *This bred defpair ; whereof fuch doubts did grow*
>   *That I gan faint, and all my courage fail.*
> *But now, my* Blage, *mine error well I fee ;*
>   *Such goodly light King David giveth me.*"

In a court like that of Henry VIII. high favour was near akin to danger and to death, and Blagge efcaped as hardly from the fires in Smithfield as from the French cannon at Landreci. In 1546, when Wriothefley and Gardiner commenced their perfecutions on the ftatute of the Six Articles, he was taken up as a "favorer of the Gofpel,"[6] and was only faved by Henry's perfonal interpofition. Fox's narrative is this :[7]

" Here would alfo fomething be faid of Sir George

---

[5] Surrey and Wyat, vol. i. p. 80.
[6] Strype's Memorials, vol. i. pt. i. p. 598.
[7] Fox's Acts and Monuments, 1135 (ed. 1546).

Blage,

Notes.

Blage, one of the King's Privy Chamber, who,
being falfely accufed by Sir Hugh Caverley, knt.
and Mafter Littleton, was fent for by Wriothefley,
Lord Chancellor, the Sunday before Anne Afkew
fuffered, and the next day was carried to Newgate,
and from thence to Guildhall, where he was condemned the fame day, and appointed to be burned
the Wednefday following. The words which his
accufers laid unto him were thefe : ' What if a moufe
fhould eat the bread ? then, by my confent, they
fhould hang up the moufe :' whereas, indeed thefe
words he never fpake, as to his life's end he protefted. But the truth (as he faid) was this, that
they, craftily to undermine him, walking with him
in Paul's Church, after a fermon of Dr. Crome,
afked if he were at the fermon. He faid, ' Yea,'
' I heard fay,' faith Mafter Littleton, ' that he faid
in his fermon, that the mafs profiteth neither for the
quick nor for the dead.' ' No,' faith Mafter Blage,
' Wherefore then ? Belike for a gentleman, when
he rideth a hunting, to keep his horfe from ftum-
bling.' And fo they departing, immediately after
he was apprehended (as is fhewed) and condemned
to be burned. When this was heard among them
of the Privy Chamber, the King, hearing them
whifpering together (which he could never abide)
commanded them to tell him the matter. Where-
upon the matter being opened, and fuit made to the
King, efpecially by the good Earl of Bedford, then
Lord Privy Seal, the King, being fore offended with
their doings, that they would come fo near him, and
even into his Privy Chamber, without his knowledge, fent for Wriothefley, commanding eftfoons
to draw out his pardon himfelf, and fo was he fet at
liberty :

liberty: who, coming after to the King's prefence, 'Ah! my pig' (faith the King to him, for fo he was wont to call him). 'Yea,' faid he, 'if your Majefty had not been better to me than your bifhops were, your pig had been roafted ere this time.' "

Fox is in error[8] when he fpeaks of Blagge as one of the Gentlemen of the Privy Chamber, a poft which he never held, and alfo in calling him at that time *Sir* George Blagge. Fox antedates Blagge's knighthood, an honour which was conferred on him in 1547, by the Protector Duke of Somerfet, whom, whilft Earl of Hertford, Blagge accompanied in the Expedition to Scotland.[9] Blagge was knighted after the fight at Muffleborough,[10] and in the fame year he and Sir Thomas Holcroft were made Commiffioners of the Mufters.[11] In 1548-9 occurred that tragedy wherein one Seymour, the Lord Admiral, fell by the warrant of his own brother, the Protector, Duke of Somerfet, himfelf deftined to fall under the fame axe. Some of the depofitions of the witneffes againft the Lord Admiral have long fince appeared;[12] thofe of the Marquis of Dorfet, the Lord Ruffell, (Privy Seal) *Sir George Blagge*, and Lord Clynton, have only recently been brought to light.[13] Blagge's evidence

---

[8] Strype's Annals, vol. ii. pt. ii. p. 419.
[9] Surrey and Wyat, vol. ii. p. lxxxiii.
[10] Holinfhed, vol. iii. p. 888.
[11] Holinfhed, vol. iii. p. 868.
[12] In Haynes' State Papers from the Burghley Collections, belonging to the Marquis of Salifbury, at Hatfield.
[13] From the State Paper Office, by Mr. Frafer Tytler in his

evidence tends to prove the criminal projects of the Lord Admiral.

In 1550 died Lord Wriothesley, at whose hands whilst Lord Chancellor, Blagge had incurred such imminent peril. His narrow escape may account for, although it cannot excuse the severity of the only remains of Blagge's writings; which are lines on the death of Wriothesley. Dr. Nott, by whom they were first printed,[14] and in whose work they may be found, says that he gives them " from the Harington MS. more from the circumstance of their having been written by one of Surrey's friends than from any merit they possess."

On the 17th June in the following year, 1551,[15] Sir George Blagge died at Stanmore in Middlesex, of which his wife Dorothy afterwards obtained a lease from Queen Elizabeth.

Sir Thomas Wyat was wont to say that he cherished three friends in particular—" Poynings for the generosity of his disposition, *Blagge for his wit*, and Mason for his learning."[16] In a letter from Lever to Ascham[17] it is said, in allusion to his loss,

his "England during the reigns of Edw. VI. and Mary." vol. i. pp. 146, etc.

[14] Surrey and Wyat, vol. i. p. xcvi.
[15] Gage's History of Suffolk.
[16] Surrey and Wyat, vol. ii. p. lxxxiii.
[17] Strype's Cheke, p. 89.

that

that England was " punifhed, as to courtfhip, by *Gentle Blage.*" [18]

---

[18] By a ftatement in Nott's Surrey and Wyat, vol. ii. p. lxv. it would feem that Blagge did not die until after his friend Wyat's execution in 1553, as he was appointed to offices previoufly held by Wyat, viz. " Keeper of the King's Meffuage at Maidftone," and " High Steward of Maid-ftone."

TABLE II.

SHEWING THE CONNEXION BETWEEN SIDNEY GODOLPHIN AND THE FAMILY OF LORD BERKELEY OF STRATTON.

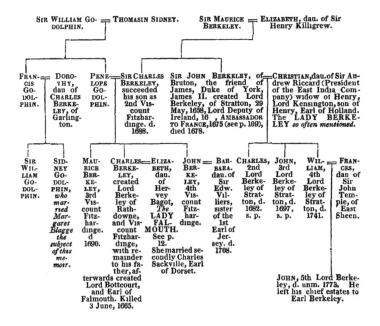

SIR WILLIAM GO-DOLPHIN. ⚭ THOMASIN SIDNEY.   SIR MAURICE BERKELEY. ⚭ ELIZABETH, dau. of Sir Henry Killigrew.

FRAN-CIS GO-DOL-PHIN. ⚭ DORO-THY, dau of CHARLES BERKE-LEY, of Garling-ton.

PENE-LOPE GO-DOL-PHIN. ⚭ SIR CHARLES BERKELEY, succeeded his son as 2nd Vis-count Fitzhar-dinge. d. 1688.

SIR JOHN BERKELEY, of Bruton, the friend of James, Duke of York, James II. created Lord Berkeley, of Stratton, 29 May, 1658, Lord Deputy of Ireland, 16 , AMBASSADOR TO FRANCE, 1675 (see p. 109), died 1678. ⚭ CHRISTIAN, dau. of Sir Andrew Riccard (President of the East India Company) widow of Henry, Lord Kensington, son of Henry, Earl of Holland. The LADY BERKE-LEY *so often mentioned*.

SIR WIL-LIAM GO-DOL-PHIN.

SID-NEY GO-DOL-PHIN, *who married Margaret Blagge the subject of this memoir.*

MAU-RICE BER-KE-LEY, 3rd Vis-count Fitz-har-dinge. d 1690.

CHARLES BERKE-LEY, created Lord Berke-ley of Rath-downe, and Vis-count Fitzhar-dinge, with re-mainder to his fa-ther, af-terwards created Lord Bottcourt, and Earl of Falmouth. Killed 3 June, 1665. ⚭ ELIZA-BETH, dau. of Her-vey Bagot, *The* LADY FAL-MOUTH. See p. 12. She married se-condly Charles Sackville, Earl of Dorset.

JOHN BER-KE-LEY, 4th Vis-count Fitz-har-dinge. ⚭ BAR-BARA, dau. of Sir Edw. Vil-liers, sister of the 1st Earl of Jer-sey. d. 1708.

CHARLES, 2nd Lord Berke-ley of Strat-ton, d. 1682. s. p.

JOHN, 3rd Lord Berke-ley of Strat-ton, d. 1697, s. p.

WIL-LIAM, 4th Lord Berke-ley of Strat-ton, d. 1741.

FRAN-CES, dau of Sir John Tem-ple, of East Sheen.

JOHN, 5th Lord Berke-ley, d. unm. 1773. He left his chief estates to Earl Berkeley.

TABLE III.

TO SHEW THE PATRONAGE EXTENDED TO MRS. GODOLPHIN BY THE DUKE OF BUCKINGHAM'S FAMILY.

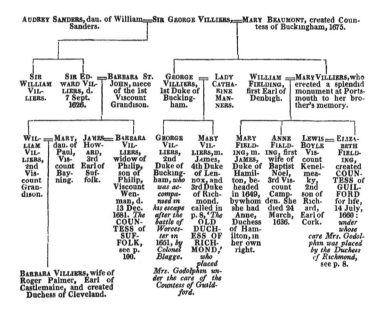

AUDREY SANDERS, dau. of William Sanders. ═ SIR GEORGE VILLIERS, ═ MARY BEAUMONT, created Countess of Buckingham, 1675.

SIR WILLIAM VILLIERS.

SIR EDWARD VILLIERS, d. 7 Sept. 1626. ═ BARBARA ST. JOHN, niece of the 1st Viscount Grandison.

GEORGE VILLIERS, 1st Duke of Buckingham. ═ LADY CATHARINE MANNERS.

WILLIAM FIELDING, first Earl of Denbigh. ═ MARY VILLIERS, who erected a splendid monument at Portsmouth to her brother's memory.

WILLIAM VILLIERS, 2nd Viscount Grandison. ═ MARY, dau. of Paul, Viscount Bayning.

JAMES HOWARD, 3rd Earl of Suffolk. ═ BARBARA VILLIERS, widow of Philip, son of Philip, Viscount Wenman, d. 13 Dec. 1681. *The* COUNTESS of SUFFOLK, *see p.* 100.

GEORGE VILLIERS, 2nd Duke of Buckingham, *who was accompanied in his escape after the battle of Worcester in* 1651, *by Colonel Blagge.*

MARY VILLIERS, m. James, 4th Duke of Lennox, and 3rd Duke of Richmond. called in p. 8, 'The OLD DUCHESS OF RICHMOND,' *who placed Mrs. Godolphin under the care of the Countess of Guildford.*

MARY FIELDING, m. JAMES, Duke of Hamilton, beheaded in 1649, by whom she had Anne, Duchess of Hamilton, in her own right.

ANNE FIELDING, first wife of Baptist Noel, 3rd Viscount Campden. She died 24 March, 1636.

LEWIS BOYLE Viscount Kinelmeaky, 2nd son of Richard, Earl of Cork. ═ ELIZABETH FIELDING, created COUNTESS of GUILFORD for life, 14 July, 1660: *under whose care Mrs. Godolphin was placed by the Duchess of Richmond, see p.* 8.

BARBARA VILLIERS, wife of Roger Palmer, Earl of Castlemaine, and created Duchess of Cleveland.

TABLE IV.

SHEWING THE DESCENT AND CONNEXIONS

OF LADY SYLVIUS.

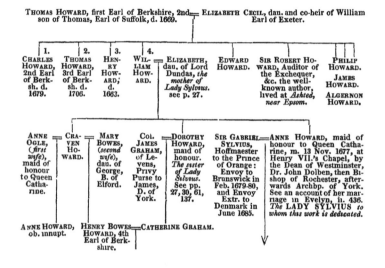

THOMAS HOWARD, first Earl of Berkshire, 2nd═══ ELIZABETH CECIL, dau. and co-heir of William
son of Thomas, Earl of Suffolk, d. 1669.   Earl of Exeter.

1. CHARLES HOWARD, 2nd Earl of Berksh. d. 1679.

2. THOMAS HOWARD, 3rd Earl of Berksh. d. 1706.

3. HENRY HOWARD, d. 1663.

4. WILLIAM HOWARD.═══ ELIZABETH, dau. of Lord Dundas, *the mother of Lady Sylvius.* see p. 27.

EDWARD HOWARD.

SIR ROBERT HOWARD, Auditor of the Exchequer, &c. the well-known author, lived at *Ashted, near Epsom.*

PHILIP HOWARD. JAMES HOWARD. ALGERNON HOWARD.

ANNE OGLE, (*first wife*), maid of honour to Queen Catharine.═══ CRAVEN HOWARD.═══ MARY BOWES, (*second wife*), dau. of George, B. of Elford.

Col. JAMES GRAHAM, of Levens, Privy Purse to James, D. of York.═══ DOROTHY HOWARD, maid of honour. *The sister of Lady Silvius.* See pp. 27, 30, 61, 137.

SIR GABRIEL SYLVIUS, Hoffmaester to the Prince of Orange: Envoy to Brunswick in Feb. 1679-80, and Envoy Extr. to Denmark in June 1685.═══ ANNE HOWARD, maid of honour to Queen Catharine, m. 13 Nov. 1677, at Henry VII.'s Chapel, by the Dean of Westminster, Dr. John Dolben, then Bishop of Rochester, afterwards Archbp. of York. See an account of her marriage in Evelyn, ii. 436. *The LADY SYLVIUS to whom this work is dedicated.*

ANNE HOWARD, ob. innupt.

HENRY BOWES HOWARD, 4th Earl of Berkshire.═══ CATHERINE GRAHAM.

TABLE V.

SHEWING THE CONNEXION BETWEEN THE
FAMILIES OF GODOLPHIN, EVELYN,
AND HARCOURT.

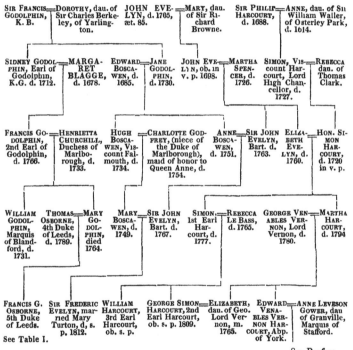

SIR FRANCIS GODOLPHIN, K. B.—DOROTHY, dau. of Sir Charles Berkeley, of Yarlington.
JOHN EVELYN, d. 1705, æt. 85.—MARY, dau. of Sir Richard Browne.
SIR PHILIP HARCOURT, d. 1688.—ANNE, dau. of Sir William Waller, of Osterley Park, d. 1614.

SIDNEY GODOLPHIN, Earl of Godolphin, K.G. d. 1712.—MARGARET BLAGGE, d. 1678.
EDWARD GODOLPHIN, d. 1730.—JANE BOSCAWEN, d. 1685.
JOHN EVELYN, ob. in v. p. 1698.—MARTHA SPENCER, d. 1726.
SIMON, Viscount Harcourt, Lord High Chancellor, d. 1727.—REBECCA dau. of Thomas Clark.

FRANCIS GODOLPHIN, 2nd Earl of Godolphin, d. 1766.—HENRIETTA CHURCHILL, Duchess of Marlborough, d. 1733.
HUGH BOSCAWEN, Viscount Falmouth, d. 1734.—CHARLOTTE GODFREY, (niece of the Duke of Marlborough), maid of honor to Queen Anne, d. 1754.
ANNE BOSCAWEN, d. 1751.—SIR JOHN EVELYN, Bart. d. 1763.
ELIZABETH EVELYN, d. 1760.—HON. SIMON HARCOURT, d. 1720 in v. p.

WILLIAM GODOLPHIN, Marquis of Blandford, d. 1731.
THOMAS OSBORNE, 4th Duke of Leeds, d. 1789.—MARY GODOLPHIN, died 1764.
MARY BOSCAWEN, d. 1749.
SIR JOHN EVELYN, Bart. d. 1767.
SIMON, 1st Earl Harcourt, d. 1777.—REBECCA LE BASS, d. 1765.
GEORGE VENABLES VERNON, Lord Vernon, d. 1780.—MARTHA HARCOURT, d. 1794.

FRANCIS G. OSBORNE, 5th Duke of Leeds. See Table I.
SIR FREDERIC EVELYN, married Mary Turton, d, s. p. 1812.
WILLIAM HARCOURT, 3rd Earl Harcourt, ob. s. p.
GEORGE SIMON HARCOURT, 2nd Earl Harcourt, ob. s. p. 1809.—ELIZABETH, dau. of Geo. Lord Vernon, m. 1765.
EDWARD VENABLES VERNON HARCOURT, Abp. of York.—ANNE LEVESON GOWER, dau of Granville, Marquis of Stafford.

See Preface.

PRINTED BY C. WHITTINGHAM, CHISWICK.

For EU product safety concerns, contact us at Calle de José Abascal, 56–1°, 28003 Madrid, Spain or eugpsr@cambridge.org.

9781108061940